37 Things To Know About Grammar

37 Things To
Know About Grammar

Matteson Claus

TRADE PAPER
PRESS

For my mom, Mary, who taught me good grammar. And for my niece, Ava, to whom I hope to pass the good grammar torch.

Turner Publishing Company
200 4th Avenue North • Suite 950
Nashville, Tennessee 37219
(615) 255-2665

www.turnerpublishing.com

37 Things To Know About Grammar

Copyright © 2010 Turner Publishing Company

Library of Congress Cataloging-in-Publication Data

Claus, Matteson.
 37 things to know about grammar / Matteson Claus.
    p. cm.
 ISBN 978-1-59652-586-3
 1. English language--Grammar. I. Title. II. Title: Thirty-seven things to
know about English grammar.
 PE1112.C56 2010
 428.2--dc22
                              2010021062

Printed in China

10 11 12 13 14 15 16 17—0 9 8 7 6 5 4 3 2 1

*The greater part of the world's troubles are
due to questions of grammar.*

~Michel de Montaigne

*I have spent most of the day putting in a
comma and the rest of the day taking it out.*

~Oscar Wilde

Contents

Introduction

Why do you really need to know anything about grammar? In a world of tweets, texts, and IMs, grammar might seem a bit irrelevant, if not completely obsolete. But what about those occasions when you need to whip out an actual sentence and you don't want to look clueless? Take this example:

> They're were Jingus Cohen the concurrer.

In case you forgot your decoder ring, I'll just translate that for you:

> There was Genghis Khan, the conqueror.

I'm so sorry to tell you that I didn't make up Jingus. He was in a sentence that came across my desk a few years ago. It took me forever to figure out what the writer was trying to say because, on top of the errors in the sentence, the topic had nothing to do with ancient warlords.

That Jingus sentence got me thinking. What happens when a gnarly sentence like that one makes its way to the boss? I can't imagine the Big Cheese spending 15 minutes deciphering a single sentence as I did. How many opportunities are lost due to bad grammar mojo?

The more I thought about it, the more I realized that there are still plenty of places where we need to use good grammar. To name a few:

- business memos
- reports
- presentations
- emails
- invitations
- love letters
- condolence notes
- that annoying "year in review" letter sent with a Christmas card

With so many chances for humiliation, messing up seems inevitable. Not true! You just need to know a few things about grammar.

Why did I write this book?

Wherever possible, I try really hard to avoid being the Jingus girl, but sometimes I need a little help. Even though I'm a writer and editor by profession, my wee brain can't contain all the grammar rules at one time. Honestly, sometimes I have to look stuff up.

The problem is that answering grammar questions can be like reading entrails to divine the future. It often involves digging through pages of mind-numbing rules praying for an answer. By the time I'm done, I usually have my cranky pants on.

There is no good reason why we should have to shovel through piles of pages for a good answer to a recurring grammar question. Why can't we chuck the stuff we'll never use and, instead, put all the good stuff in one easy-to-use book? It turns out we can!

I've noticed that there are certain grammar gremlins that rear their ugly heads a lot. As it turns out, when I boiled down the questions and problems I see and hear most, I wound up with just 37 things you really need to know. Now I'm putting them all together in one handy-dandy place to share with you.

Why is this book different from other grammar books?

It's exclusive. Think of *37 Things* as the hot nightclub of grammar books: only certain grammar gremlins are allowed inside. If you're looking for the complete set of grammar rules for the English language, you won't find it here. I included only the stuff that regular people might actually need as they go about their daily routines.

Think pizza, not Brussels sprouts. I understand why people tend to approach grammar with about the same enthusiasm as kids dining at an all-you-can-eat Brussels sprouts buffet. Yes, this book is good for you. But there's a reason why this book isn't called 37 Things That Make You Cringe.

In this book, grammar isn't a Brussels sprout. Grammar is like pizza: you pick and choose what you need to create the best result. Whether you're going for simple, plain-cheese grammar or a grammar supreme, you're in charge of making something yummy that will please you.

I promise not to make you diagram a sentence. I'd love to know who decided that grammar had to be such a serious, dry topic. Words should be fun. If you're looking for a stodgy, uptight approach to grammar, you won't find it here.

No shovel is necessary. You won't find endless, tedious lessons where you have to dig for answers until your brain oozes out your ears. Instead, you'll find a quick explanation of the hows and whys of each thing, and then some examples so that you can see the thing in action.

It's arranged by elves. Okay, the book was arranged by me, but I'm short, so think of me as an elf. Although the Things may look willy-nilly, there is a modicum of method to my madness. Instead of giving you a huge pile of rules, the book is grouped by things that go together. For example, you'll find all the stuff relating to pronouns grouped together (Things 6-10). And, the Things start with the basic grammar building blocks, the parts of speech, and unfold into how to put those building blocks together correctly.

Slang is not the tool of the devil. No grammar Nazis here. You'll find several examples of slang in this book. Sometimes slang is good. Sometimes it's fun. But sometimes you need to refrain, and to do that, you need to be able to tell the difference between slang and proper usage.

So, how should you use this book, anyway?

As a grammar refresher. Been a long time since you've even thought about grammar? If you feel as if you've become lost in the Land of Text Messages, feel free to use this book as a gentle reminder of what the Land of Actual Sentences is like. I suggest using the book like a "word-a-day" calendar, except that you read one grammar thing a day.

As a reference guide. Can't keep *there*, *they're*, and *their* straight? No problem. Just go to Thing 36 and check out the examples. Is where to put the apostrophe driving you nuts? Easy breezy, there's a whole Thing on that, too. Anytime you need a quick answer, you'll have the 37 Things right at your fingertips.

For pointers. As a bonus, some of the Things include "Seriously, people . . ." boxes. These boxes highlight specific grammar abuses that drive readers to swear in disgust and despair. Use these boxes as helpful pointers.

By the way, in case you were wondering . . .

What is grammar? In case you were wondering, grammar is kind of like therapy for words: it is the study of words, their functions, and relationships. Fortunately, there's no ginormous hourly therapy fee to contend with. (Yes, this is a grammar book and I just said "ginormous." Twice. I told you I'm not a grammar Nazi.)

What rules? English grammar looks as if it was assembled by drunken pirates on a dare. It has all these crazy rules. For extra fun, it just flat out refuses to follow them sometimes. Consider yourself warned: although grammar rules tend to apply in general, you can almost always find an exception to any rule.

For example, if you pay attention, you'll see me breaking some of the rules in how I write this book. You'll see me do naughty things like use slang and sentence fragments here and there. Generally, that kind of thing is frowned upon, but because I'm doing it on purpose, not accidentally, and for a specific effect (I'm writing in a very informal, conversational tone), I can get away with it. In moderation.

What is a style guide? Speaking of exceptions, style guides are full of them. A style guide sets out the rules of how you're supposed to write for a particular publication or company. So, for example, if you're a student writing something for the social sciences, you are likely to need the APA style guide. But if you're a journalist writing for a newspaper or magazine, you may wind up following the *Chicago Manual of Style.*

Not everyone will have to deal with style guides—it depends on what you're writing and for whom you're writing it. I mention style guides because if you do have to use them, they can affect how you write. I'll tell you the rules for commas, but a style guide may ask you to handle commas differently. If you are writing for a specific publication, you should check to see if the publisher follows a particular style guide. If you're writing a bunch of reports, it helps to know if your company has a style guide.

Why can't we just write like we talk? A gap has always existed between how we speak and how we write, but the gap seems lately to be growing wider than ever. Speaking is like the beta version of our communications: you've got some structure there and it basically works, but it's got technical issues. Writing is the gamma version: you've had time to clean up the mistakes, giving you a more polished product. The amount of polish varies with the type of writing you're doing—some types of writing are more formal than others. But in the end, writing is supposed to be more technically accurate than speaking, because you've had time to edit what you say.

By the way, if you're a fiction writer, the exception to this rule is when you're writing dialogue. To effect realism, feel free to mangle the language just the way people do when they speak. (Exception to the exception: doing so sparingly generally works better.)

Why not just use spell check? It's a nice backup. But don't trust it to make your writing look good. Basically, spell check can catch some errors, but it will miss a ton of others. We'll have a longer chat about the pitfalls of spell check in Thing 34: *Rely on cruise control to drive your car, and you're an accident waiting to happen. Rely on spell check to edit your writing, and you'll crash and burn just as surely.*

The bottom line

You know what? Good grammar isn't absolutely necessary all of the time. But when you need it, you'd better be able to grab it and use it right. To do that, there are certain things you should know about grammar so that you can tell the difference between what's right and what's wrong.

This book is meant to help you present yourself better. If you want a raise, your writing should show that you deserve it. If you're the boss, it's kind of hard to earn the respect of your employees if your memos look as if they were written by a third-grader. Even if you just want your friends to take you seriously, good grammar will allow you to present yourself much better than a Jingus jumble.

Let's put the groovy back in grammar and have a look at some grammar things!

The 37 Things

~ 1 ~

The parts of speech are the ingredients you need to cook up a good sentence

What's the most basic thing about grammar? The parts of speech.

Do you suspect that the word flirting with your nouns is supposed to be snuggling with your verbs, but you're not sure why? Knowing your parts of speech will help you identify that word and put it in its place.

I think of the parts of speech like the parts of a pizza. To make a good pizza, you have to know your pizza parts, from the dough to the toppings. To make a good sentence, you have to know what kinds of words you're using, from the nouns to the verbs. With pizza and parts of speech, your goal is to assemble the parts into a juicy whole where everything goes together with mouthwatering results.

Getting comfy with the parts of speech will help to assemble your good grammar pizza. If it's been awhile since you reviewed them, have a nice visit with the list below. You can also refer back to the list anytime you feel bewildered by the ingredients of your sentence.

- **noun:** names a person, place, or thing
  examples: pizza, cheese, tomato

  Why you care: Want toppings on your pizza? You need to name them. That means using some nouns.

  > I bought **cheese** and a **tomato** for my **pizza**.

- **pronoun:** takes the place of a noun
  examples: she, it, them

  Why you care: It gets really old saying the same noun or proper noun over and over.

  > **Without pronouns: Carla** said the **pizza** was good. **Carla** said the **pizza** was gooey.

  > **With pronouns:** Carla said the pizza was good. **She** said **it** was gooey.

- **verb:** shows action or a state of being
  examples: devoured, dripped (action verbs), was (state of being)

Why you care: If you want to tell what's happening or what's being done, you're going to need a verb of some sort. Want to torture your friends with stories of the fantastic dinner you had?

> **Without verbs:** You the pizza. It cheese. The pizza awesome.
>
> **With verbs:** You **devoured** the pizza. It **dripped** cheese. The pizza **was** awesome.

* **preposition:** links a noun to another word and gives you information like location, direction, and time. This information helps you understand the relationship between the words in the sentence.

examples: inside (location), up (direction), after (time)

Why you care: Prepositions help glue your sentence together. They are like the cheese that connects the toppings to the sauce and the dough.

> **Without prepositions:** The pizza boy walked the driveway, she welcomed him the house.
>
> **With prepositions: After** the pizza boy walked **up** the driveway, she welcomed

him **inside** the house.

- **adjective:** describes or modifies a noun or pronoun
  examples: large, thick

  Why you care: A lot of the time, just naming something isn't going to do the trick. You need to give more information. To order the perfect pizza, you'll want to describe it.

  > I'd like to order a **large** pizza with a **thick** crust.

- **adverb:** describes or modifies a verb, adjective, or other adverb
  examples: suddenly, too, far

  Why you care: Adverbs answer questions like **when, where,** and **how.** Want to talk about where you're getting your next pizza? Use an adverb.

  > He realized **suddenly** it wasn't **too far** to the pizza parlor.

- **conjunction:** joins words, phrases, and clauses
  examples: but, and, or

Why you care: Conjunctions will help you link your thoughts together. Want to add or exclude things from your pizza? Use some conjunctions.

> I know you think I'm nuts, **but** I want both olives **and** anchovies, **or** just artichokes on my pizza.

- **interjection:** shows emotion
  examples: Hey! Ah! Oh!

   Why you care: Want to yell at that dude who cut you off in traffic on your way to get the pizza? You need an interjection.

> **Hey!** Can't you see I'm on my way to get a pizza?

You see interjections a lot in poetry. This poem, while tragically lacking in pizza references, has two interjections:

First Fig

My candle burns at both ends;
It will not last the night;

*But **ah,** my foes, and **oh,** my friends—*
It gives a lovely light.

~Edna St. Vincent Millay,
"A Few Figs from Thistles," 1920

What about a, an, and the?

They are called articles. Articles are not considered a separate part of speech, because they are classified as adjectives.

Now that you've got your parts of speech sorted out, you're ready to start baking some grammatically gorgeous sentences.

~ 2 ~

You can't be in the past, present, and future at the same time, and neither should your sentence

I'm fairly certain you are not a Time Lord. As a result, your ability to time travel is limited to your writing. Using different verb tenses allows you to visit the past, present, and future. But generally, you don't want to do it all in the same sentence. Check this out:

> I **am walking** down the street, and I
> **was blown** away by that bad grammar.

First, I **am walking.** This is present tense. This is happening right now. Then, in the second half of the sentence, I **was blown** away. Suddenly, this isn't happening now. It is happening in the past.

Randomly changing tenses confuses your reader. Do it often enough in your writing, and you can make your reader's head explode. Not only is this unfortunate for your reader and messy for you, but your writing will suffer and no one will want to read it.

Switching tenses ruins an otherwise perfectly good sentence. Take, for example, an email sent on International Talk Like A Pirate Day.

> **Pirate:** Arr, I be waitin' fer a chance to talk like a pirate. I was sad I had to wait so long.

Unfortunately, this poor pirate wannabe hasn't quite gotten the hang of pirate speak. You'll notice the first sentence is fine, but alas, the second sentence switches tenses and ruins all the fun.

Whether you're writing normally or like a pirate, the rule is the same. Decide what tense you're writing in and stick to it.

Regular and irregular verbs. As I said, the rules of grammar sometimes look as though they were designed by drunken pirates, and using the different verb tenses can be a tense experience. There are rules, but with all that pirate influence, there are also rule breakers.

The majority of verbs are **regular verbs** that follow the rules. To get to the past tense, mostly you add a **-d** or an **-ed** and you're done.

Me matey and me **keelhauled** that scallywag fer tryin' to steal from us.

But, because this is English and it's a wonky language, some of our past-tense verbs look as though they've been sharing the rum with the pirates. In case you were wondering, we call these **irregular verbs.** You don't really need to know how to name them, you just have to know how to use them.

The verb "to drink" is a good example of an irregular verb.

The pirate **drinks** all the rum. *(present)*

(He's drinking it right now. If you hurry, you might still grab some for yourself.)

The pirate **drank** all the rum. *(past)*

(He already drank it. The rum is gone. Give it up; you're not getting any.)

You were going to get an adult beverage but found that the pirate **had drunk** all the rum. *(past participle)*

(Oh man! He got all the rum before you even got there. You need to step up your game or get

used to living a rum-free existence.)

It's this last form of the verb that seems to cause the most trouble. It doesn't follow the regular verb rules. In fact, the word **drunk** looks artificial. You've probably even heard someone say it should be **had drinken** or **had drunken** instead of **had drunk.** I'm so sorry to tell you that **drunk** is correct. It's just an irregular verb.

Irregular verbs are needy. They don't like to be alone. So you always use them in combination with a helping verb, like "has" or "had." Here's a partial list of some common irregular verbs to help you out if you get confused.

Present	Past *(likes to be alone)*	Past Participle *(needy; won't work without a helping verb like "had")*
drink	drank	drunk
fall	fell	fallen
freeze	froze	frozen
give	gave	given
go	went	gone

have	had	had
ring	rang	rung
ride	rode	ridden
run	ran	run
shrink	shrank	shrunk
sing	sang	sung
speak	spoke	spoken
steal	stole	stolen
swim	swam	swum
wear	wore	worn
write	wrote	written

If you ever have questions about your verbs, don't be shy about looking them up in a dictionary or on a reliable Web site. I do, when I get confused! Some irregular verbs look so bizarre that I can't help checking to make sure I've got the right word.

Seriously, people ...

Even pirates knew better than to have **drug** things to their ships. The word **drug** is *not* the past tense of "to drag."

> **Nay:** The pirate found himself wishing he **had drug** the wench to the ship.

> **Aye:** The pirate found himself wishing he **had dragged** the wench to the ship.

> **Aye:** The pirate took the **drug** to clear up the unfortunate reminder of his last trip to port.

(For more on drag vs. drug and other commonly confused words, see Thing 35.)

— 3 —

Just because you say you shoulda, doesn't mean you should have written it that way

Shoulda, coulda, woulda and **should of, could of,** and **would of** are good examples of the gap between how we talk and how we're supposed to write.

Coulda, shoulda, woulda are slang.

> Guy said, "I **woulda** gone home. In fact, I probably **shoulda** gone home. But really, who **coulda** resisted *that?* I'm only human you know."

Should of, could of, and **would of** are just plain wrong. Don't use them.

> Dude said, "Yeah, you **should of!** Bonehead, I **could of** come to get you, but you probably **would of** refused to leave."

But always in formal writing, and usually in informal writing, both **shoulda** and **should of** are grammatically incorrect. When you're writing, use **should've, could've, would've, should have, could have,** and **would have.** If Guy sent Dude an email, it might look like this:

> You're right. I **should've** left. If I had gone home, I **could have** and **would have** avoided the whole mess.

Obviously, not all writing is the same. Dialogue is one area where you can throw many writing rules out the window. If you're writing dialogue and you want it to seem authentic, don't make the grammar perfect. Use all the shouldas and wouldas that you need to breathe life into your characters.

To sum up:

> **No:** shoulda, coulda, woulda; should of, could of, would of
>
> **Yes:** should've, could've, would've; should have, could have, would have

$-4-$

Active verbs provoke and stimulate. Passive verbs are boring

Avoid humdrum writing! Go for the active voice over the passive voice.

What's the difference between using the active and passive voices? Active writing is kind of like coffee for verbs: it gives them some wang and makes your reader come to attention. Passive writing is kind of like beer for verbs: it mellows and flattens them out to the point where your reader might fall asleep.

Being active or passive in your choice of verbs is just like being active or passive in any other area of your life. It really comes down to whether you're going to be a big wussie with wishy-washy verbs, or you're going to man up with verbs that have chutzpah.

Check this out:

> **Passive:** The door was slammed by her.
>
> **Active:** She slammed the door.

Granted, neither of these sentences is going to win a Pulitzer. Still, the active sentence has some sass to it, whereas the passive is dull. And the passive sentence puts the emphasis on the door, not on the woman. In this case, the emphasis should be on the woman.

Passive sentences use some form of the verb "to be," either as the main verb or as a helping verb. With a little rearranging and some thought, you can often pick stronger, clearer, more active ways to say what you want.

> **Passive:** The mischievous monster **was** on the stairs, waiting for her to leave the house. She **was tripped** by the crafty critter. Before she knew it, the sidewalk **was** under her nose.
>
> **Active:** The mischievous monster **lurked** on the stairs, waiting for her to leave the house. The crafty critter **tripped** her. Before she knew it, she **lay sprawled** on the sidewalk.

You can't always avoid using the passive voice. If you don't know who is doing the action in the sentence, using the passive voice is a convenience.

We know who did the action (active voice): Later, Kyle **gave** her a can of critter spray.

We don't know who did the action (passive voice): Later, a can of critter spray **was given** to her.

Now before the grammar Nazis start foaming at the mouth, let me be clear. Using the passive voice is *not* a grammatical error. However, it can weaken your writing and muck up the clarity.

Grammar purists may also argue that voice is a matter of style, not grammar. I disagree. Since voice is basically about picking the right form of a verb, I think it has as much to do with grammar as style. And, since my job is to show you groovy grammar things, I can't really excuse not mentioning it to you.

As long as you're aware that you are using the passive voice and you realize what it does, then party on. But if you're just using it because you don't know any better, or worse, because you're too lazy or chicken to pick a strong verb, then you need to switch to the active side of the Force.

— 5 —

Prepositions are like the Mafia: to avoid trouble, know who they are

If you want to have good grammar, you've got to make friends with the prepositions. For such little words, these guys can create quite a bit of chaos. Prepositions are the David that will bring down your grammar Goliath.

Prepositions and subjects. Prepositions love to hide the subject of your sentence. If you can't recognize the preposition, it's really easy to lose track of your subject. That, in turn, will mess up your verb. Before you know it, your whole sentence is out of whack and the preposition is having a good laugh at your expense. *(For more on subject-verb agreement, see Thing 19.)*

Prepositions and pronouns. Can't decide if it should be **I** or **me?** Look for a preposition lurking nearby to solve the puzzle. Prepositions can help determine which pronoun to use. *(To understand the whole **I** vs. **me** thing, see Thing 7.)*

Prepositions and the end of a sentence. You can end your sentence with a preposition if you want **to**. It is commonly supposed that prepositions are those things which you should never, ever end a sentence **with**. Although I have the sneaking suspicion that ancient grammar teachers are rolling over in their graves, this is *not* the rule and hasn't been for some time. If you want to end with a preposition, that's just fine, particularly if whatever you're writing is informal. For formal writing, avoid doing it too much. It can make your writing look sloppy.

Not sure what a preposition looks like? Check out the list of some common prepositions below.

about	before	except	of	through
above	behind		off	to
across	below	for	on	toward
after	beneath	from	onto	
against	beside		outside	under
among	between	in	over	
around	by	inside		until
at		into	past	up
	despite			upon
	down	like	since	
	during			with
		near		within
				without

21

Don't worry. I'm not going to insist that you memorize the list of prepositions, but you should try to become familiar with them because they are wily. Being able to recognize prepositions will definitely make your writing life easier.

Seriously, people . . .

Don't go adding extra prepositions if you don't need them. You run the risk of looking as if you don't know the difference between slang and proper English. Although extra prepositions can add character to the way people speak, they are just wrong when it comes to writing. (The exception, as usual, is when you're writing dialogue.)

> **Spoken:** Where are you **at?**
> **Written:** Where are you?
>
> **Spoken:** I don't know where my money went **to.**
> **Written:** I don't know where my money went.

— 6 —

Pronouns are obsessed with matching

There are a few things you need to know about pronouns (five, in fact). But first, and maybe most important, is that these guys are all about the matching.

As I mentioned earlier, a pronoun takes the place of a noun. A pronoun is like a stand-in stepping in to give the noun a break. The pronoun isn't there to create a whole new role for itself. Its job is to do the same thing as the noun it's replacing. If the pronoun doesn't want to get fired, it had better be really good at matching the noun.

Ways to match your pronouns.

- **Pronouns must match their nouns in number.**
  If the noun is singular, so is the pronoun.
  If the noun is plural, so is the pronoun.

Simple, right? Not so much. It's one of the most common

mistakes that writers make.

> **No:** The United States thinks **they** have all the best Santas.

> **Yes:** The United States thinks **it** has all the best Santas.
>
> *(A country is always considered an **it** not a **they**.)*

- **Pronouns also have to match each other in number.**
  If you say **they,** then you have to say **their,** not **his.** If you say **he**, you have to say **his,** not **their**.

  > **No:** When **they** got hot waiting for Santa, **they** removed **her** coat.

  > **Yes:** When **they** got hot waiting for Santa, **they** removed **their** coats.

- **Pronouns must match in person.**
  Basically, pick a point of view and stick with it. So, if you're writing from a first-person point of view ("I did such and such"), then stay in first person. Otherwise, your sentences start to look schizophrenic.

  > **No:** Should **a person** take the time and effort to wait in line for Santa, **you** expect a good visit.

Yes: Should **a person** take the time and effort to wait in line for Santa, **a person** expects a good visit.

Yes: Should **you** take the time and effort to wait in line for Santa, **you** expect a good visit.

- **Pronouns must match in gender.**
  If it's a male, then use **he.** If it's a female, then use **she.**

  No: Bill took great pride in **her** Santa costume.

  Yes: Bill took great pride in **his** Santa costume.

  No: Sarah knew **he** would never look at chocolate Santas the same way.

  Yes: Sarah knew **she** would never look at chocolate Santas the same way.

- **One vs. you: pronouns must match each other.**
  Generally speaking, you should choose **you** over **one** when you're writing informally. However, whichever you pick, stick with it.

  No: If **you** want to eat the elves'

Christmas Cheer Chocolates, **one** should go ahead.

Yes: If **you** want to eat the elves' Christmas Cheer Chocolates, **you** should go ahead.

Yes: If **one** wants to eat the elves' Christmas Cheer Chocolates, **one** should go ahead.

When pronouns don't match. Pronouns that don't do their jobs well can cause a real mess. Check out this excerpt from a Christmas card:

Well, I'm so sorry to tell you that there's no annual photo of Honey with Santa this year. Honestly, I don't care what Santa and the Elves at the Mall said. **He** was being ridiculous. If **a person** is going to be a Santa, **you** should accept the risks that come with the job. No way am I paying Santa to dry-clean **her** suit.

Sure, Honey ate a few Christmas Cheer Chocolates, but those Elves are totally out of line to say she ate all the Christmas Cheer in **his** bowl. That had nothing to do with it. If **one** knows anything about children, **you** would know Santa shouldn't have jostled Honey so much. And, **her** stinky reindeer certainly didn't help matters. It's no wonder poor Honey spewed Christmas Cheer all over Santa.

Let's take this bit by bit.

We're having problems matching in **number.**

Honestly, I don't care what **Santa and the Elves** at the Mall said. **He** was being ridiculous.

*(Santa and the elves are **they** not **he,** since there's more than one of them.)*

Sure, Honey ate one or two Christmas Cheer Chocolates, but those **Elves** are totally out of line to say she ate all the Christmas Cheer in **his** bowl.

*(Since Elves is plural, it should be **their** not **his.**)*

Here, we're having problems matching in **person.**

If **a person** is going to be a Santa, **you** should accept the risks that come with the job.

*(**A person** is the third-person point of view, whereas **you** is the second-person point of view. In order to match the point of view of the rest of the card, stick with **you**.)*

Now, we can't keep our **genders** straight.

> No way am I paying **Santa** to dry-clean **her** suit.
>
> *(Santa is a dude, so it should be **his** not **her**.)*

> And, **her** stinky reindeer certainly didn't help matters.
>
> *(Since I'm thinking the reindeer belong to Santa, not Honey, it should be **his** reindeer.)*

And now, we're having problems matching **one** vs. **you.**

> If **one** knows anything about children, **you** would know Santa shouldn't have jostled Honey so much.
>
> *(Either **one** or **you** is okay technically, so long as you're consistent. Since it says **you** at the beginning of the card, then it should continue to say **you**, not **one**.)*

28

Here is what the letter should look like when written correctly:

Well, I'm so sorry to tell you that there's no annual photo of Honey with Santa this year. Honestly, I don't care what Santa and the Elves at the Mall said. **They** were being ridiculous. If **you** are going to be a Santa, **you** should accept the risks that come with the job. No way am I paying Santa to dry-clean **his** suit.

Sure, Honey ate one or two Christmas Cheer Chocolates, but those Elves are totally out of line to say she ate all the Christmas Cheer in **their** bowl. That had nothing to do with it. If **you** know anything about children, **you** would know Santa shouldn't have jostled Honey so much. And, **his** stinky reindeer certainly didn't help matters. It's no wonder poor Honey spewed Christmas Cheer all over Santa.

So, remember to match your pronouns. Not only will your pronouns be happy, but your writing will be much clearer.

Seriously, people . . .

Yous is not a word. With all love and respect for regional dialects, **yous** isn't an actual pronoun, and you shouldn't use it in your writing. Sure, **yous** adds a flavorful regional dialect if you're writing dialogue. You can also use **yous** when you're speaking, if you're so inclined. But otherwise, please, oh please, leave it out of your writing.

Whether it's *I* or *me* is the difference between dishing it out and taking it

Have you ever gone nuts trying to figure out whether to use **I** or **me, who** or **whom?** Well hop off the crazy train because I've got some help for you.

Did you know that pronouns come in different types? Well, the whole **I** or **me** thing comes down to whether your pronoun is a **subject** or an **object.**

- Subjects do the action. They dish it out.

- Objects receive the action. They take it.

It works like this:

Subject	Object
I	me

you	you
he	him
she	her
it	it
we	us
they	them
who	whom
whoever	

Some straightforward examples. We get off easy with **you** and **it** because the subject and object are the same.

You should have seen **it**.
*(**You** is the subject, and **it** is the object.)*

It would have seemed hilarious to **you**.
*(**It** is the subject, and **you** is the object.)*

But we have to pay attention to all the other pronouns because they differ.

Subject: They robbed the bank, then rushed outside to get away.

Object: But, their horses had deserted **them.**

In this example, **they** is the subject of the first sentence, the person doing the action, which is why we're using **they** instead of **them**. In the second sentence, we're using **them** because **them** doesn't do the action, **them** receives it.

Where things get confusing. Please keep in mind that we're talking about grammatically correct writing. We needn't speak this way, but this is the way we should write.

- **no prepositions**
  Suppose you have a sentence like this one:

> Honestly, I think I make a better robber than **they.**

> Honestly, I think I make a better robber than **them.**

Which is it? I have a simple trick to help you out. Sentences like this are comparing things—the word **than** tips you off to the comparison. The trick is to remember that these sentences have an unspoken verb after the pronoun. Just add it in, and you'll have your answer.

> Honestly, I think I make a better robber than **they** *make.*

33

> Honestly, I think I make a better robber
> than **them** *make.*

Obviously, the answer is **they.** It can seem a little weird, but it's correct. Try another one:

> They looked more confused than **I,** and they were the ones robbing the bank.
>
> They looked more confused than **me,** and they were the ones robbing the bank.

Now add in the unspoken verb:

> They looked more confused than **I** *did*, and they were the ones robbing the bank.
>
> They looked more confused than **me** *did*, and they were the ones robbing the bank.

Yup, weird, but **I** is correct.

- **prepositions**
They're baaaack! Remember how I told you in Thing 5 that prepositions can cause all sorts of misery? Well, in

my experience, the majority of the pain and suffering with pronouns is a result of prepositions.

Prepositions are the reason why I grow hoarse shouting at my TV "to *whom!*" (So far, it hasn't helped.)

> If the pronoun comes **after the preposition,** use the objective, not the subjective, spelling.
> *(That's when you pull out the **to whom.**)*

I find that the following prepositions cause quite a bit of pronoun pandemonium:

- **to** (to whom)
- **for** (for whom)
- **of** (of whom)
- **with** (with whom)
- **by** (by whom)

Want to know why it's *to **whom** it may concern?* It's because the pronoun **whom** comes after the preposition **to.** That means the pronoun has to be an object, not a subject.

- **compounds**

When you have a pronoun plus another word, it can be difficult to figure out which pronoun to choose.

The robber and **him** couldn't find any other horses.

The robber and **he** couldn't find any other horses.

The insider's trick for this kind of situation is to take away the other words and look at the pronoun by itself.

~~The robber and~~ **him** couldn't find other horses.

~~The robber and~~ **he** couldn't find other horses.

Now you can see that the correct answer is **he.** Try another one:

You could have knocked Scarlett and **me** over with a feather when they stole that camel.

You could have knocked Scarlett and **I** over with a feather when they stole that camel.

Isolate the pronoun:

You could have knocked ~~Scarlett and~~ **me** over with a feather when they stole that camel.

> You could have knocked ~~Scarlett and~~ **I**
> over with a feather when they stole that
> camel.

Now you can see that the correct answer is **me.**

Choosing the wrong pronouns can make your writing look amateurish. Handle them with care and your writing will look polished and professional.

— 8 —

If they are out to get you, it helps to know who "they" are

Pronouns are not spies. They should not have secret identities. On the contrary, it should always be clear what noun your pronoun is replacing.

A pronoun that loses track of its noun is kind of like a child losing track of its parent. The pronoun gets confused and all sorts of chaos ensues.

Unclear pronouns cause misery. Don't believe me? Say you're obsessed with dating a supermodel and you get this bit of news:

> Yesterday, we interviewed Serena, the serial killer, and Giselle Bundchen, the supermodel, and **she** said that **she** thinks you're hot.

Hold up! Who thinks you're hot? Giselle or Serena? Either you need to prepare for a night on the town or a flight to a hideaway, quick. If only we could tell whom the **she** refs to. But we can't because the pronoun is unclear.

Say you love actors and your assistant leaves you this note:

> Viggo Mortensen and Jeffrey Dean
> Morgan both called while you were out.
> **He** is only in town tonight and wants to
> know if you can have dinner. Call **him**
> back asap.

Are you kidding me? Call which of them back? You fire your assistant for forgetting whom you're supposed to call and for not writing down a phone number. Then you torture yourself over who your dinner date could have been. If he doesn't call back, you'll never know, because it's unclear who the **him** is.

You can also have a clarity problem if you let your pronouns get overzealous. Put too many pronouns in a row and your reader will lose track of the original nouns. Your best bet is to keep some of the nouns and just sprinkle in the pronouns to add a bit of variety to your writing.

Bad example:

> Dear Giselle:
>
> Mr. Smith sent this message through
> his assistant. **He** would like you to

know **he's** out of the country, not his
mind. Due to a recent mix-up, **he**
unexpectedly had to leave **it**.

Is Mr. Smith or the assistant out of the country? Mr.
Smith unexpectedly had to leave his mind? I'm thinking this
kind of information is not conducive to getting a date with a
supermodel.

Better example:

Dear Giselle:

The following message is forwarded from
Mr. Smith's assistant:

Due to a recent mix-up, Mr. Smith
unexpectedly had to leave the country.
He should, however, be returning
immediately. Mr. Smith sends **his**
apologies for having missed your visit,
and hopes to reschedule at your earliest
possible convenience.

Much better. Now we have a nice mix of nouns and pronouns
and everything is clear.

Grammarians call the word a pronoun refers to its "antecedent." You can easily avoid all this confusion and misery by keeping the relationship between your pronouns and their antecedents clear!

— 9 —

Who, that, and which, while pesky, are not worth any nail-biting

Who, that, and **which** can all be used as pronouns. There seems to be a lot of confusion about how to pick among the three. In particular, there is a lot of confusion between **that** and **which.**

First, let me say that this is one of those wishy-washy rules. People like to fuss over it. Honestly, if you mix up **that** and **which** it's not the end of the world. But since it's a question that comes up a lot, I think I should at least mention it.

Who. **Who** is the easiest to use of the three. **Who** refers only to people.

> **No:** The lead guitarist is the one **that** used so much hairspray his head got stuck to his mic stand.

> **Yes:** The lead guitarist is the one **who** used so much hairspray his head got stuck to his mic stand.

That and which. **That** and **which** both refer to groups or things. The confusing part comes in knowing how to choose between them. The basic idea goes like this:

- **That** is a must-have!

  Use **that** if what you're talking about is essential for the meaning of your sentence. Look at the section of your sentence with the **that.** If you take out **that** and its clause, does the sentence have the same meaning?

  > According to the spokesperson for Huge Hair, only hair ***that*** *had been sprayed with an entire can of their hairspray* could have stuck in such a manner.

  We need the "that had been sprayed with an entire can of their hairspray" to tell us specifically what kind of hair we're dealing with here. If you take "that had been sprayed with an entire can of their hairspray" out of the sentence, you lose vital information and it changes the meaning. So in this case, you'd chose **that** not **which.**

Here's another helpful tip: clauses beginning with **that** do not need commas around them.

- **Which** is optional.

  Use **which** if taking out the clause doesn't change the meaning of the sentence.

  > While executing his signature "whip and flip" head toss, the guitarist accidentally whacked his head on the stand, **which** was his favorite.

  If you take out "which was his favorite" you don't lose any meaning from the sentence. Granted, you lose a nice descriptive detail, but the meaning of the sentence remains intact. Thus, **which** not **that** is the better choice.

Here's another helpful tip: clauses beginning with **which** need commas around them.

Used incorrectly:

  > When the guitarist tried to yank his head back, the mic stand, **that** gleamed brightly, came with it.

  *(This isn't crucial information and it doesn't add meaning—so **which** should be used.)*

The guitarist lost his balance and crashed into the bass player, **that** was standing right next to him.

*(The bass player is a person, and thus a **who**, not a **that** or **which**.)*

The bass player grabbed for the amp **which** was behind him, but missed.

*(There were several amps onstage, and this tells us which specific amp he grabbed, so it's must-have information—**that** should be used.)*

The men went down in a tangle, **that** made the audience laugh.

*(The laughter is a nice detail, but not essential to the main meaning of the sentence—**which** should be used.)*

The roadies, **that** were laughing so hard they were crying, were ultimately forced to hack through the guitarist's hair in order to remove the mic stand.

*(Roadies are people, and thus a **who**, not a **that** or a **which**, is needed.)*

Used correctly:

> When the guitarist tried to yank his head back, the mic stand, **which** *gleamed brightly,* came with it. The guitarist lost his balance and crashed into the bass player, **who** *was standing right next to him.* The bass player grabbed for the amp **that** *was behind him,* but missed. The men went down in a tangle, **which** *made the audience laugh.* The roadies, **who** *were laughing so hard they were crying,* were ultimately forced to hack through the guitarist's hair in order to remove the mic stand.

The main thing with **who, that,** and **which** is to make sure you get your **who** right. Try to keep your **that** separate from your **which,** but don't stress over it.

– 10 –

Indefinite pronouns are definitely dastardly

Indefinite pronouns hate to be too specific. They still take the place of nouns. But they refer in general to people, places, and things.

> **Definite:** Everyone knew Jimmy, John, and Robert had trashed the hotel room. **They** had a history of doing such things.

*(We know who **they** are.)*

> **Indefinite:** Of course, their manager insisted that **anyone** at the party could have done the damage.

*(**Anyone** is an indefinite pronoun. We don't know anything about the people involved.)*

Singular or plural? Indefinite pronouns will mess with you because they're sneaky. Many of them look plural, but are actually singular. In fact, most of the time, they are singular. But not always!

Three of the biggest troublemakers are **everyone, everybody,** and **everything. Every** is the source of the mischief. **Every** *sounds* as if it should mean more than one, a whole bunch. A sane person would think that words containing **every** would, therefore, be plural.

Ah, but remember: English grammar was, we suspect, assembled by drunken pirates. **Every** is actually an adjective that means "being **each** or being **one** of a group." So, even though it sounds as if it should be plural, it's singular . . . and so are all its offshoots.

Indefinite pronouns can make you look inept by making you choose the wrong verb. *(For more on subject and verb agreement, see Thing 19.)*

> **No: Everybody** I know **were going** to that party at the hotel.

> **Yes: Everybody** I know **was going** to that party at the hotel.

> **No:** I thought I could I do what **everyone** else **were doing.**

> **Yes:** I thought I could do what **everyone** else **was doing.**

No: They say **everything happen** for a reason, but I still don't see the "higher purpose" behind my parents making me miss the party of the decade.

Yes: They say **everything happens** for a reason, but I still don't see the "higher purpose" behind my parents making me miss the party of the decade.

Check out the indefinite pronouns below to see what's singular and what's plural:

Singular

anybody	each	neither	one
anyone	either	nobody	
anything	everybody	no one	somebody
	everyone	nothing	someone
	everything		something

Plural

both	few	many	several

Singular and Plural. Some indefinite pronouns can be either singular or plural, depending on how you use them in a sentence. I'm telling you straight out, this particular rule is hard.

| all | any | most | none | some |

When you use any one of these words to mean a portion of something, then you need to look at the noun that comes after the **of.**

If the noun is singular or uncountable (like sugar, dirt, or rice), then the verb is singular.

> **No: Most** of the *window* **were** smeared with cake.

> **Yes: Most** of the *window* **was** smeared with cake.

*(In this case, the noun **window** is singular, so the verb is also the singular **was.**)*

> **No: Some** of the *champagne* **were** sprayed on the hotel walls.

> **Yes: Some** of the *champagne* **was** sprayed on the hotel walls.

*(You can't count **champagne,** so the verb is the singular **was.**)*

If the noun is plural, then so is the verb.

No: None of the *people* **was** upset by the food fight.

Yes: None of the *people* **were** upset by the food fight.

*(The noun **people** is plural, so the verb is also the plural **were**.)*

Indefinite pronouns can be a real pain. Instead of letting them give you a headache, I suggest getting to know the few pronouns that are definitely plural. There are far fewer of them and knowing them will help to keep you from getting confused.

Seriously, people . . .

One of the truly awkward things about the English language is its lack of a gender neutral pronoun. Thus, if we don't know the gender, we have to say "he or she thought" or "his or her dishtowel." Awkward, unwieldy, but alas, grammatically correct.

So, for example, you may write:

> **Everybody** was thrilled to get **their**
> coats and flee before the cops came.

Sadly, that's just plain wrong. Correctly written, the sentence would be:

> **Everybody** was thrilled to get **his or
> her** coat and flee before the cops came.

Everybody is singular, so you shouldn't use **their,** which is plural. As we learned in Thing 6, pronouns have to match each other in number, and the singular **everybody** doesn't match the plural **their.** That means if you use everybody, you're stuck using **he or she.** I know it's icky, but *technically* it is correct.

But wait! Here's the thing: if you go around writing "he or she" all the time, you're going to sound snooty. So, I'm going to recommend you use discretion and consider the options.

- Option A: If it's informal writing, like a quick email to a friend, use **their** anyway. If you do go that route, be consistent and don't suddenly switch back to **he or she.** I recently read a nonfiction book where the author chose to use **their.** It worked just fine because she wrote in a very informal, conversational style and because she was consistent.

- Option B: If it's formal writing, a report for example, suck it up and go with **his or her.**

- Option C: If you can't stand the way it looks when it's grammatically correct (and who could blame you), try rewriting the sentence to get around it:

    > **The people at the party** were thrilled to get **their** coats and flee before the cops came.

- Option D: If you're writing something that's long and includes numerous and unrelated references, you can switch off. Try using **she** for one set of references, then **he** for the second, **she** for the third, and so forth.

- Option E: Pick one gender, either he or she, and just use that one consistently.

— 11 —

Want to tell your sumptuous sweeties how smokin' hot they are? You're going to need some adjectives

Adjectives are fun. They make our writing tantalizing and tasty. Instead of just saying what something is (noun) and what it's doing (verb), we use adjectives to fill in the juicy details.

> **Plain:** The bubble exploded. Gum dripped from her hair.

> **With adjectives:** The **enormous** bubble exploded. **Slimy** gum dripped from her **ruined** hair.

Adjectives and commas. Sometimes you may use several adjectives in a row. If you do, you may need to separate your adjectives with commas. *(For more on commas, see Thing 24.)*

How can you tell if you need a comma? If you can put the word **and** between the adjectives and it makes sense, then add a comma. If not, leave it alone.

No: Stringy slimy gum dripped from her **ruined** hair.

Yes: Stringy, slimy gum dripped from her **ruined** hair.

*(You could say **stringy and slimy**, so add the comma.)*

No: Purple, bubble gum dripped from her **ruined** hair.

Yes: Purple bubble gum dripped from her **ruined** hair.

*(You wouldn't say **purple and bubble**, so no comma.)*

Adjectives and hyphens. Now things get a bit trickier. People tend to have a really hard time figuring out what to do with hyphens in general, but specifically they like to torture their adjectives with them. *(For more on hyphens, see Thing 27.)*

If you have two adjectives that work together, expressing a single thought, then they should be hyphenated.

Huge, shiny tears streamed down her **gum-covered** face as she howled with **riotous**, **belly-shaking** laughter.

(Since gum-covered and belly-shaking express single thoughts, they are hyphenated. Huge and shiny are two separate things, so they aren't hyphenated, but they are separated with a comma.)

Basically, you want to avoid confusing your reader. Check out this example:

> "I'm a rogue demon hunter," said Wesley.
> "What's a rogue demon?" asked Cordelia.

~From TV's Angel, "Parting Gifts," season one, episode 10, written by David Fury and Jeannine Renshaw

Cordelia heard **rogue-demon** when Wesley meant **rogue hunter.**

I'm a rogue-demon hunter means "I'm a dude who hunts a type of demon called a rogue."

I'm a rogue demon hunter means "I'm a rogue, a maverick, and I hunt demons."

See how important that tiny hyphen can be?

- If the adjective comes **before** the noun, you hyphenate. If it comes **after,** you don't.

> **Before:** Even though it was a **low-budget** movie, the quality of the brain-sucking slugs was surprisingly good.
>
> **After:** Even though the movie had a **low budget**, the quality of the brain-sucking slugs was surprisingly good.

Don't let a verb that reminds you of an adjective trick you into hyphenating it.

> **Adjective:** After the movie was released, he made a **follow-up** call to see if the slugs were a bang or a bust.
>
> **Verb:** He decided **to follow up** on the call that said the slugs were a sensation.

- Keep an eye out for the **"well + word" combos,** such as **well respected.** These get messed up a lot. Again, if they come after the noun or verb, then do not hyphenate. If they come right before the noun, add the hyphen.

> **Yes:** I don't care what you say, I saw that movie because it is **well written.**

> **Yes:** I don't care what you say, I saw that movie for the **well-written** scenes.

> **Yes:** He totally denied he went on the date with the actress, just because she was **well known** for that slug movie.

> **Yes:** He totally denied he went on the date with her, just because she was that **well-known** actress from that slug movie.

• Mind those **adverbs.** To add one more fly to the ointment, don't hyphenate adverbs ending in -*ly* that are next to adjectives. They like to cuddle.

> Those **incredibly cute** slugs will eat your eyeballs for a snack.
> *(Since* **incredibly** *is an adverb, and* **cute** *is an adjective, no hyphen is necessary. Let them cuddle in peace.)*

Enjoy the way adjectives infuse your writing with color and texture. Just remember to use your commas and hyphens wisely so that your readers can enjoy the fun without getting confused.

— 12 —

Grab some adverbs to tell your boss how, when, where, and why you're late

I believe the road to hell is paved with adverbs, and I will shout it from the rooftops.
~Stephen King, *On Writing*

Although I don't necessarily agree with Mr. King that adverbs are evil, they can be problematic. The good thing about adverbs is that they increase our ability to describe things. Where adjectives are limited to describing nouns, adverbs can describe verbs, adjectives, and even other adverbs. Generally, adverbs help you tell how, when, and where.

Say you're stuck in a traffic jam and you decide to email your boss from your phone. Using adverbs will help you to explain why, instead of staring at your gray cubicle walls, you're staring at the gray car in front of you.

Dear Mr. Bossyboots:

I'm emailing you from my car. Don't worry: I'm not driving **carelessly.** I carpool **daily** and I'm not driving **today.** I was sitting here **anxiously** chewing my thumbnail as we chugged **sluggishly** up the freeway, and I thought I'd better drop you a note. We haven't gone **very far** in the last half hour because everyone is **carefully** navigating through an accident ahead of us. **Apparently,** a truck from Craig's Crocodile Crib flipped over, and **now** there are baby crocodiles **merrily** cavorting up and down the freeway. I'm sorry for the delay and will arrive as **soon** as I can.

The adverbs allow you to tell your boss important **when, why,** and **how** information that will, hopefully, keep you from being fired.

Too many adverbs. The biggest problem with adverbs is that you can rely on them too much. If you do, your writing can become lazy and unclear. Adverb skeptics would argue that none of the adverbs in the email above are actually needed.

For example:

> I was sitting here **anxiously** chewing my thumbnail as we chugged **sluggishly** up the freeway, and I thought I'd better drop you a note.

I could replace **anxiously chewing** with **gnawing** because **gnawing** is arguably a stronger word choice than **anxiously chewing.** I could also delete **sluggishly** since **chug** already implies slowness. The result would be a more concise sentence. Now it reads:

> I was sitting here gnawing my thumbnail as we chugged up the freeway, and I thought I'd better drop you a note.

Be careful where you put them. Putting your adverb in the wrong place can change the meaning of your sentence.

Check this out:

> He **nearly** slept through the entire movie.
> *(He didn't quite fall asleep.)*

He slept through **nearly** the entire movie.

(He fell asleep and missed most of the movie.)

His girlfriend said she **almost** left him there halfway through the film.

(She was going to leave, but she didn't.)

His girlfriend said she left him there **almost** halfway through the film.

(She got up and left about midway through the film.)

The other guys in the carpool laugh at him **only** when he tells them about his dates.

(The guys just laugh at him about his dates, not about anything else.)

The other guys in the carpool laugh **only** at him when he tells them about his dates.

(None of the other guys gets laughed at. It's just him.)

Watch out for double negatives. You've probably heard that you shouldn't use two negative words together, but did you know that some adverbs count as negatives? Watch out for sneaky negative adverbs like **hardly, barely,** and **scarcely.** You want to avoid using these words with other negatives like **no, none, nothing, never,** or **not.** Check it out:

> **No:** I **can't scarcely** remember when I wasn't stuck in this car.
>
> **Yes:** I **can't** remember when I wasn't stuck in this car.
>
> **Yes:** I can **scarcely** remember when I wasn't stuck in this car.

(Remember, **can't** *is a contraction standing for* **cannot.** *Since* **not** *is a negative and so is* **scarcely,** *you've got to pick one. Don't use both.)*

> **No:** I've heard of being knee-deep in alligators, but I **barely never** thought I'd experience it literally.
>
> **Yes:** I've heard of being knee-deep in alligators, but I **barely ever** thought I'd experience it literally.
>
> **Yes:** I've heard of being knee-deep in alligators, but I **never** thought I'd experience it literally.

No: So far, I've had **hardly no** contact with reptiles, and I'd like to keep it that way.

Yes: So far, I've had **hardly any** contact with reptiles, and I'd like to keep it that way.

Yes: So far, I've had **no** contact with reptiles, and I'd like to keep it that way.

Not all adverbs end in -ly. It's true that many adverbs end in -*ly*. However, many adverbs don't end in -*ly,* such as **less, far,** and **well.**

Similarly, just because a word has an -*ly* doesn't necessarily mean it's an adverb. Granted, this is the exception, not the rule. But be aware that words like **lovely, friendly,** and **lonely** are adjectives, not adverbs.

Adverbs aren't an all-or-none proposition. If you're judicious in your use of adverbs, they can help you to communicate more effectively. The bottom line with adverbs is to use them thoughtfully and sparingly.

Seriously, people . . .

I do agree with Mr. King about adverbs and dialogue. Stop with all the adverbs! If you're writing dialogue, stick to "he said" and "she said." Leave off the adverbs, as in "he said huffily" or "she said stormily." I particularly love this example from King's *On Writing:*

> "You got a nice butt, lady," he said **cheekily.**

Okay, not all adverbs used in dialogue are this bad, but overuse of them is a bad thing. It's also lazy. We should be able to tell how someone says something by relying on the rest of the sentence. Check out this example:

> He staggered against the wall and said, "Good Lord! What's that smell?"

But if you really think you need to show how someone says something, try using a verb before resorting to an adverb.

> "Good Lord! What's that smell?" he wheezed.

～ 13 ～

Sure, that band rocks hard, but to decide if it's good, better, or the best, you have to know what you're comparing it to

Shall I compare thee to a summer's day?
Thou art more lovely and more temperate
~William Shakespeare, "Sonnet 18"

Y ou don't have to be Shakespeare to make a good comparison. You do, however, need to be able to tell the difference between **good, better,** and **best.**

Mess up your comparisons and you'll end up with painful errors like **more quicklier.** Such a tiny mistake can take your writing from awesome to appalling in two small words.

Regular comparisons. The key to awesome comparisons is knowing how many things you're comparing. Most words follow this pattern:

> **For comparing two things:** use **more** or **less,** or words ending in -er.

For comparing more than two things: use **most** or **least,** or words ending in -est.

For example:

Base word	Two things	More than two things
hot	hotter	hottest
fine	finer	finest
groovy	groovier	grooviest

Even the majority of slang follows this pattern. For example:

Base word	Two things	More than two things
skanky	skankier	skankiest
sketchy	sketchier	sketchiest
rockin'	more rockin'	most rockin'
bangin'	less bangin'	least bangin'

Irregular Comparisons. Of course, it can't be that easy, because this is English. Irregular comparisons are where we get into trouble. They don't follow the regular patterns because, heck, that'd just make life too simple.

Here's a list of some common irregular comparisons for your reference:

Base word	Two things	More than two things
bad	worse	worst
far	farther	farthest
good	better	best
little	less	least
many, much, some	more	most

*Which words use **more, most, less, or least**?* This is one of those wishy-washy rules that make things hard.

Some words feel that it's way cooler to use **more-most** or **less-least** instead of adding -er or -est. These words *generally* hang out only with words having *three or more* syllables. Sadly, there are exceptions. Sometimes **more** and its cousins will allow words with two syllables to hang out with them.

Not sure which way to go? Just look it up in the dictionary to be sure.

Base word	Two things	More than two things
quickly	more quickly	most quickly
excited	less excited	least excited

| extraordinary | more extraordinary | most extraordinary |
| radical | less radical | least radical |

There are two big no-nos for using **more-most** or **less-least.**

• Don't add **more, most, less,** or **least** to words that already have -er or -est.

> **No:** At first she thought that might be the **most scariest** groupie she'd ever seen. But she decided the groupie was **less scarier** than the one she'd seen earlier.

> **Yes:** At first she thought that might be the **scariest** groupie she'd ever seen. But she decided the groupie was **less scary** than the one she'd seen earlier.

• Don't add **more, most, less,** or **least** to irregular comparisons. Irregular comparisons may seem a bit wacky but they get along just fine on their own. Don't try adding extra words to help them—they don't need it.

> **No:** Man, you played that guitar solo way **more better** than that dead dude used to play it.

Yes: Man, you played that guitar solo way **better** than that dead dude used to play it.

Fortunately, making comparisons is actually kind of fun, once you get the hang of it. Good comparisons are a very helpful tool for you and your reader because comparisons help to illustrate what you're trying to say.

~ 14 ~

There's no need to feel bad because you become badly confused trying to do a good job using your adjectives and adverbs well

Ah, the age-old battle between **good** and **well, bad** and **badly.** It really comes down to whether you need an adjective (**good** and **bad**) or an adverb (**well** and **badly**).

Since both adjectives and adverbs describe things, you can see where it'd be easy to get them mixed up.

A helpful hint: adjectives are exclusive daters. They hang out only with nouns and pronouns. If what you're describing isn't a noun or pronoun, use an adverb. Here are some more tips to help you choose wisely.

Good vs. Well

Good is an adjective. In general, **good** answers the question "what kind." **Well** is an adverb. In general, **well** answers the question "how."

> **No:** She had **well** habits.
>
> **Yes:** She had **good** habits.

*(The adjective **good** tells you what kind of habits she has.)*

> **No:** Her habits usually served her **good** during flu season.

> **Yes:** Her habits usually served her **well** during flu season.

*(The adverb **well** tells you how her habits served her.)*

- **Where people tend to get stuck:**

If you're talking about your health, you feel **well**. Any other time you talk about how you feel, you feel **good**.

For example:

> **Q:** How do you feel? Are you still hocking up a lung?
> **A:** I feel **well**.

> **Q:** How do you feel? Are you still worried about the end of the world as we know it?
> **A:** Oddly, I feel **good**.

Bad vs. Badly

Bad is an adjective and **badly** is an adverb.

No: Is it a **badly** thing that I told her she looks like 10 miles of **badly** road?

Yes: Is it a **bad** thing that I told her she looks like 10 miles of **bad** road?
*(**Bad** is an adjective in both cases, telling you what kind of thing and what kind of road.)*

No: She reacted **bad** when I told her.

Yes: She reacted **badly** when I told her.
*(**Badly** is an adverb, telling you how she reacted.)*

Seems simple enough, but of course there's a catch.

• **Where people tend to get stuck:**

Pain-in-the-Adjective Verbs: **taste, smell, look, feel,** and **sound**

With these *verbs that apply to the five senses,* mostly you need to use the adjective **bad,** *not* the adverb **badly.** Check this out:

What do you mean, that doesn't **taste bad?** Oh man, are you still sick? I thought you said you didn't **feel bad.**

You still **sound bad** to me. How long has it been since you've had a bath? You **smell** really **bad.** Actually, you **look bad,** too.

Although our friend here could use some help with his bedside manner, his grammar is correct.

- **The exception**

The only time to use **badly** in place of **bad** with these verbs is if you want to use these verbs actively.

I taste badly.

Meaning: I am physically unable to use my sense of taste correctly.

I feel badly.

Meaning: I am physically unable to use my sense of touch correctly.

Sound . . .

There's no such expression as **sound badly.** Period. We can, however, listen badly and hear badly.

I smell badly.

Meaning: I am physically unable to smell things the way I'm supposed to.

I look badly.

Meaning: Something is wrong with my sight.

◈

Really, choosing between **good-well** or **bad-badly** is about taking the time to think about your word choice. If you pause to take a look at your sentence and check the context, you should have no problems making a good choice!

Seriously, people . . .

If you're feeling sick, sorry, or sad, then you feel **bad.** You do *not* feel **badly.**

If you do feel **badly,** you should probably see a neurologist, to get your sense of touch working properly. In the meantime, please be careful not to accidentally hurt yourself.

$-15-$

Putting your modifier in the wrong spot is like putting your shoe on the wrong foot. It feels awkward and looks kind of wacky

Modifiers describe other words. They can be single words, like adjectives or adverbs, or they can be whole phrases and clauses.

When you're dealing with only one word, it's fairly simple to make sure you stick it in the right spot. But when you're dealing with a whole phrase, it's really easy to accidentally misplace your modifiers.

Want to avoid these mistakes? **Put your modifier next to the word it modifies.**

Modifiers are like small children: they need to hold hands with the words they modify. Otherwise, they wander off and all sorts of crazy antics follow.

Misplaced modifiers

> The sun shone on the coffin, **which was unusually bright.**

According to this example, the coffin is unusually bright. I'm pretty sure the sun is what's shining brightly, not the coffin. The modifying phrase *which was unusually bright* is in the wrong place. It should be right next to the noun it's modifying, which in this case is **sun.** The sentence should read:

> The sun, **which was unusually bright,** shone on the coffin.

Misplaced modifiers can make your writing really confusing to read. They can also provide a lot of unintended humor for your readers. This can be unfortunate if you're writing something with a serious tone, say a condolence card.

> Dear Friends and Family,
>
> I'm writing to inform you that Uncle Howard has passed on with a heavy heart. At the time he passed, I understand he was fishing with his dog in his favorite plaid shirt. He was always happiest on that boat with his dog and Aunt Em, which was his prize possession. Flowers can be sent to the funeral home in his name.

Oh my. Poor Uncle Howard had a heavy heart? The dog was wearing Howard's favorite plaid shirt? Aunt Em is Howard's prize possession? There's a funeral home named after Howard?

Eek! See what happens when your modifiers don't hold hands with their nouns? Here's how it should appear:

> Dear Friends and Family,
>
> With a heavy heart, I'm writing to inform you that Uncle Howard has passed on. At the time he passed, I understand he was in his favorite plaid shirt, fishing with his dog. He was always happiest on that boat, which was his prized possession, with his dog and Aunt Em at his side. If you would like to send flowers, send them in his name to the funeral home.

Dangling modifiers. Personally, when I misplace my modifiers, I tend to leave them dangling. Dangling phrases are still misplaced, but they're hanging off the beginning or end of your sentence.

> **Still hanging in the closet,** she noticed his plaid shirt.

According to the example, she is still hanging in the closet. It's a safe bet that what I meant to say was that the shirt is hanging. The sentence should look like this:

> **Still hanging in the closet,** his plaid shirt caught her notice.

or

> She noticed his plaid shirt, **still hanging in the closet.**

Sure, dangling modifiers can be amusing. But say you just spent a week crafting a report that is supposed to inspire your boss to give you a raise, only to hear peals of laughter coming from his office when he reads it. Ouch.

> In summary, even in the midst of shopping for a funeral, the lingerie was bought by the women. Pooped as they were, the colorful undergarments still provided these gals with a boost. With their silky, soft feeling, women can't help pass up these unmentionables. Uplifting while practical, I feel lingerie is a guaranteed sale.

The lingerie was shopping for a funeral? The colorful garments were pooped? The women feel silky soft? Am I uplifting and practical, or is the lingerie? I think what I meant to say in my report was this:

> In summary, even in the midst of shopping for a funeral, the women bought the lingerie. The colorful garments still provided a boost to these gals, pooped as they were. With their silky, soft feeling, these unmentionables couldn't be passed up by the women. Uplifting and practical, lingerie is a guaranteed sale, I feel.

I wouldn't worry too much about your modifiers when you're writing a first draft. But if you keep them in mind while you edit, you can save yourself some embarrassment.

― 16 ―

OMG r u 4 real? IMHO u must 86 this habit B4U get axed

Translation: *Oh my God, are you for real? In my humble opinion, you must eighty-six (quit using) texting language before you get fired.*

Think a good man is hard to find? Between the Internet, instant messaging, and texting, it's even harder to find an actual sentence these days. This is a problem for a few reasons.

Although I'm going to talk about communications on the job, really this applies to any kind of formal writing.

Your business memo should not look like a text message. Text messages absolutely have their place. But the whole thing with text lingo is to save money by using as few characters as possible. This does not encourage us to use actual words. It does not promote the use of actual sentences. And it certainly doesn't make for good grammar.

If text messages were confined to our phones, things would be fine. But somehow text-messaging shorthand has slithered its way into everything from school reports to business emails.

If you don't want to get an F or get fired, you're going to need to use real sentences and real words. *(For more on crafting a complete sentence, see Thing 17.)*

Your business email should not look like an instant message. I know emoticons are fun, but they do not belong in your business emails. Again, in a professional email there should be real words and complete sentences.

You should also refrain from using IM acronyms (many of which are also used in texting). Telling the Powers-That-Be that you're LOL at that joke they made, or signing off with a jaunty TTFN, is mostly unwise.

Also, unlike IMs, you should absolutely proofread professional emails before you send them.

Your business report should not necessarily look as if it came off the Internet. I hope you're fully aware that you can't always trust what you see on the Internet. But maybe it hasn't occurred to you that this doesn't just apply to content, but also applies to *how* things are written. Web writing has its own set of conventions and styles that don't always have to do with decent grammar. Just because it's written on the Internet, doesn't mean it is written correctly.

Your business communications should contain something other than buzzwords. Now, I know businesses have their own jargon. That's fine. If your company likes buzzwords, go ahead and use them. But you really shouldn't just string together random business words that you see on the Internet or that you've heard in meetings. Even if you're writing a report, it should actually make sense.

Some examples:

Text message:

c u l8r

IM:

OMG! still ROTFL about last night ☺ boss here ☹ c u 2nite TTFN

Personal email:

Heya,
Last night was SO much fun. I had a

blast. Gotta run, the boss is coming this way. But looking forward to seeing you later. ☺
Hugs!

Business email (informal):

Hi Larry,

Thanks again for including me in the client meeting last night. What a delight to find out he had such a great sense of humor!

I'm looking forward to the dinner this evening.

Thanks,
Bill

Business email (formal):

Dear Mr. Alexander:

Per our conversation last night, I am RSVPing for tonight's dinner.

It was a pleasure to meet the client

in such a relaxed setting last evening.
I look forward to the opportunity to
explore our investment strategies
further at tonight's event.

Sincerely,
Bill Anderson

Business report (with jargon):

In conclusion, we had an excellent
brainstorming session with the client.
With the client's focus on accountability,
it's obvious that we will need to be
proactive in presenting our strategies at
tonight's dinner. I recommend we push
the envelope as much as possible.

Choose the format that works best for the situation. In
the end, no matter what format you're using, you want to
communicate clearly.

— 17 —

Not a complete sentence.
This is a complete sentence

For a long time now, the gap between how we speak and how we write has been getting wider. Now with texts and tweets encouraging us to use shorter and shorter phrases, people seem to be forgetting how to craft a proper sentence. The complete sentence misses you and wishes you would visit more often!

I promise you that writing a complete sentence can be quite simple. To make a complete sentence, all you need is a subject and a verb. Really, you learned this in first grade, remember?

> See Dick.
> See Dick run.
>
> Dick tripped.
> Jane laughed.

So what's the problem?

Beware the sentence fragment. Enter the nefarious sentence fragment. A fragment is an expert deceiver because it often mimics the way we talk. So, when you hear it in your head, the fragment may sound like a sentence. Alas, it's not! Fragments are really just snippets of a sentence.

> Office policy clearly states that
> employees should walk. At all times.
> Not run. Therefore, it's Dick's own fault
> that he slipped. Falling in front of the
> watercooler. And spilling the water
> all over himself. In fact, he created a
> hazardous situation for his coworkers.
> Not to mention for himself.

If you read this example out loud, it makes some sense. That's the way people talk—in a mix of sentences and short phrases. But, chances are, your reader won't be reading your writing out loud. As a result, that example can read like a bunch of gobbledygook.

Look at the example again. All of the italicized parts are fragments. Not one of them has both a subject and a verb.

> Office policy clearly states that
> employees should walk. *At all times.*
> *Not run.* Therefore, it's Dick's own fault
> that he slipped. *Falling in front of the*

> watercooler. *And spilling the water
> all over himself.* In fact, he created a
> hazardous situation for his coworkers.
> *Not to mention for himself.*

To correct the problem, you need to adjust and combine the incomplete bits to make them into whole sentences. Here's one possible solution:

> Office policy clearly states that
> employees should walk *at all times.*
> They should *not run.* Therefore, it's
> Dick's own fault that he slipped, *falling
> in front of the watercooler,* where he
> *spilled the water all over himself.* In
> fact, he created a hazardous situation
> for his coworkers, *not to mention for
> himself.*

Now the phrases have been integrated so they're parts of complete sentences.

Why do you care? Seasoned writers sometimes use fragments to good effect, but for most of us, writing in fragments can make comprehension really difficult for the reader. Sure, *you* know the words you have omitted that would complete your thought, but your reader can only guess. The reader can't hear the thought in your head, which is where it remains if you don't express it completely.

The inability to write a proper sentence can also make you look very unprofessional (and possibly illiterate). I once worked for someone who couldn't tell the difference between a fragment and a complete sentence. Employees needed a cryptographer to read this person's reports, letters, and memos. We secretaries did what we could to improve whatever came across our desks, but I remember thinking that if I were a client receiving one of these proposals, I'd be horrified and wouldn't give the company my business.

You can keep your communications short and sweet and still use complete sentences! You'll get your point across better, and you'll look smarter and more professional while you're doing it.

Seriously, people . . .

Sure, emails are, by nature, a fairly casual form of communication. But please, if you're emailing someone professionally, you need to use complete sentences or you're going to look bad. You can still keep it short, but your workmates deserve full sentences.

Personal email:

> Man, got the report. Could suck worse. Not by much.

Professional email:

> I received the report and am reading it now. I wouldn't say that it's bad, but it could use some work.

— 18 —

Please be gentle with our wee brains separate each of your ideas clearly so our heads don't explode

W hat's wrong with the title above? It's an example of a run-on sentence. You create a run-on when you cram too much into the same sentence without proper punctuation. Thing 18 should actually look like this:

> Please be gentle with our wee brains. Separate each of your ideas clearly so we can understand them.

or:

> Please be gentle with our wee brains; separate each of your ideas clearly so we can understand them.

or:

> Please be gentle with our wee brains, separating each of your ideas clearly so we can understand them.

You can fix a run-on sentence by:

a) breaking up the single sentence into multiple sentences.

b) adding a semicolon.

c) changing one part of the sentence into a dependent clause, often by adding a comma and a conjunction like *and* or *but*.

Comma splices. Ah, but wait! Be careful with that comma thing, or you might accidentally create a comma splice error. Look at this:

> Please be gentle with our wee brains,
> separate each of your ideas clearly so
> we can understand them.

Know why this is wrong? Because I forgot to add the **and** after the comma. You can't glue two sentences together with a comma alone. You also need a conjunction.

You correct a comma splice error the same way you correct a run-on sentence. Either break up the sentence, add a semicolon, or create a dependent clause. Check this out:

Run-on sentence:

> My cat's brain is bigger than mine he
> knows it.

Comma splice error:

> My cat's brain is bigger than mine, he
> knows it.

Correct:

> My cat's brain is bigger than mine. **He**
> knows it.

or:

> My cat's brain is bigger than mine; he
> knows it.

or:

> My cat's brain is bigger than mine, **and**
> he knows it.

Whoops! Check out this common mistake:

> My cat's brain is bigger than mine; **and**
> he knows it.

Why is the sentence wrong this time? Because I added
the semicolon *plus* the **and.** Unlike a comma, a semicolon
is strong enough to glue two sentences together all by itself.

Either add the comma plus the **and,** *or* add the semicolon, but not both.

Overall, the thing to remember is that you want to give each individual idea its own space. Trying to cram too much into a sentence is like trying to cram too many people into a party. It starts off well, but by the end, it's a crowded, confused mess.

Seriously, people . . .

It's just wrong to squish every last thing you possibly can into one sentence. It's not as if there's a shortage of periods, so there is no reason for you to hoard them.

> **Overstuffed:** Recently, we did a scan of my cat's brain, and though the doctors were surprised, I was relieved to see that there's some basis for my assumption that my cat's brain is bigger than mine, as was shown by the details on the scan, which were really quite interesting and illuminating.

One way to reorganize it: Recently, we did a scan of my cat's brain. Though the doctors were surprised, I was relieved to see that there's some basis for my assumption that my cat's brain is bigger than mine. The details on the scan were really quite interesting and illuminating.

Please, spread your thoughts out instead of mashing as much as you can into a single sentence.

— 19 —

If your sentence is a marriage, then you are its therapist. To save the sentence, you must get the subject and verb to agree

Trying to convince your subjects to get along with your verbs can be quite problematic, but it's as important as helping any couple resolve their differences. Subjects and verbs that don't agree ruin the harmony of your sentences.

Matching subjects with verbs looks simple.

> single subject = single verb
> plural subject = plural verb

Your subjects, however, can be surprisingly coy.

Subject hide-and-seek. The main problem, as I see it, is that subjects like to play hide-and-seek. Sometimes what you think is the subject of the sentence really isn't.

> The color of the bridesmaids' dresses makes the girls look as if they're about to barf.

What's the subject here? It looks as though it should be **dresses,** but it's not. The subject is **color.**

- **Beware the prepositions!**

How did this happen? The prepositions are back again! **Dresses** can't be the subject because it's part of the prepositional phrase *of the bridesmaids' dresses.* **Dresses** is too busy being the object of the preposition **of** to take on the job of subject.

Here we are again with those little prepositions causing all sorts of mayhem. Whenever you try to find the subject of a sentence, just remember to keep an eye out for pesky prepositions. If you find a word you think is the subject, but it's part of a prepositional phrase, think again. The overwhelming majority of the time, your subject is not going to be part of a prepositional phrase.

The exception: Ah, you knew there had to be one! If your prepositional phrase comes after a word that indicates a portion, like *some, percent, all,* or *part,* then look at the noun that comes after the preposition. If the noun is singular or uncountable (like sugar, dirt, or rice), the verb should be singular. If the noun is plural, so is the verb. *(For more on singular and plural indefinite pronouns like **some, all,** or **none,** see Thing 10.)*

No: All of the *sequins* **is** dizzying.

Yes: All of the *sequins* **are** dizzying.

No: None of the *fringe* **are** necessary.

Yes: None of the *fringe* **is** necessary.

- **Play matchmaker.**
  Look at this sentence again:

> The **color** of the bridesmaids' dresses
> **makes** the girls look as though they're
> about to barf.

Since **color** is the subject and it is singular, then the verb **makes** has to be singular as well. Ta-dah! Everyone agrees now.

*(Yeah, I know, **makes** ends in **-s** which you might think would mean it was plural. But remember, verbs don't form plurals by adding an **-s** to the end.)*

Either-or, neither-nor. So what happens if you have a wonky subject, like **either** or **neither?** Then things get really interesting.

- **If the subject is just *either* or just *neither,* easy breezy. Your verb is singular.**

> **No: Either** of the moms **know** better than to use sequins and fringe.

> **Yes: Either** of the moms **knows** better than to use sequins and fringe.
>
> *(Ignore the prepositional phrase* of the moms.*)*

> **No:** However, **neither** of them **have** much input in the matter.

> **Yes:** However, **neither** of them **has** much input in the matter.
>
> *(Ignore the prepositional phrase* of them.*)*

- **If the subject is compound and includes *either-or,* or *neither-nor,* choose the noun that's closest to the verb (meaning the subject after the *or* and *nor*).**

> **No:** *Either* you *or* **I are** going to have to say something.

> **Yes:** *Either* you *or* **I am** going to have to say something.

> **No:** *Neither* the best man *nor* the **bridesmaids is** going to wear day-glo orange fringe if I can help it!

> **Yes:** *Neither* the best man *nor* the **bridesmaids are** going to wear day-glo orange fringe if I can help it!

Indefinite pronouns. You know how we talked about indefinite pronouns in Thing 10? Well, indefinite pronouns provide another opportunity for wackiness with your subject-verb agreements.

Remember that many indefinite pronouns look plural but are actually singular. *(For a reference list, check out Thing 10).* If your subject is a singular indefinite pronoun, your verb should be single, too.

> **Somebody is** taking bets on whether the bridesmaids will trip over the enormous bows on their dresses.

If your indefinite pronoun is plural, so is your verb.

> **Many** of us **are** hoping the wedding goes smoothly despite the outrageous outfits.

Remember that every sentence can be broken down to a core of just a subject and a verb. Since they are the center of any sentence, it's really important that the subject and verb agree.

– 20 –

Because the road to hell is not actually paved with sentences starting with *and* or *because,* go ahead and use them

Many of us had it hammered into our heads that you absolutely, positively *never* start a sentence with **and** or **because.** I was warned of dire consequences if I started my sentences with **and** or, worse, the dreaded **because.**

Guess what? I'm delighted to tell you that this is no longer a hard and fast rule. To encourage developing writers to write sentences that needn't rely on transition words, teachers may want to limit the use of **because** or **and.** That's fine. But grammatically, there's no real reason not to use these words to start a sentence.

Go easy with your newfound freedom:

- Starting too many sentences with **and** or **because** will make your writing look sloppy and too conversational. It's also just plain lazy. Your best bet is to use a variety of transition words and phrases.

- It's not nice to make your teacher's head explode. Do you have a teacher or boss who likes the old rule? Then, by all means, follow their instructions when turning in a paper or report. That way, their heads will stay intact and you won't suffer their wrath for having disobeyed.

- If you get too fast and loose with your **because** usage, you can unintentionally write a bunch of incomplete sentences. Be careful that you don't accidentally wind up with a sentence fragment instead of a complete sentence.

Examples:

> **No: And** yesterday I heard this new song. **And,** it didn't really blow my skirt up. **And** then I heard it again later. **And** I thought it was pretty groovy the second time around.

*(I used **and** way too many times.)*

> **Yes: Yesterday** I heard this new song. **And,** it didn't really blow my skirt up. **But** then, I heard it again later. **Surprisingly,** I thought it was pretty groovy the second time around.

*(Now I have a variety of transition words, but I still got my **and** in there.)*

No: Because it's silly.

(This is a sentence fragment, not a complete sentence.)

Yes: Because it's silly, the song grew on me.

(Now it's a complete sentence.)

Feel free to indulge in an occasional **because** or **and** at the beginning of your sentences. Just don't get carried away.

— 21 —

Promote sentence Zen: create balance in your sentences

Ever read a sentence that seems off, but you can't put your finger on why? Chances are that the items in the sentence are not evenly balanced, or parallel.

Parallels are like an equation. Both sides should match.

> **No:** You can hunt either the undead or sleep all day.

*(Here, the word **either** sets up the equation, where the first part, the clause starting with **either,** must match the second part, the clause starting with **or.** You can't hunt sleep all day!)*

> **Yes:** You can either hunt the undead or sleep all day.

> **Yes:** Either you can hunt the undead or you can sleep all day.

Lists. One of the most common ways to unbalance your sentences is to put items in a list that don't match. Check this out:

> **No:** The vampire hunter taught us **staking, slaying,** and **how to run away.**

The items in this list are not stated the same way, and as a result, the sentence feels awkward. Right now, there are two verbs and a verb phrase (grammarians call them gerunds and infinitives, but we needn't go there). Try this instead:

> **Yes:** The vampire hunter taught us **staking, slaying,** and **retreating.**

> **Yes:** The vampire hunter taught us how to **stake, slay,** and **retreat.**

If one thing in your list is a verb, then the whole list needs to be made of the same kind of verb. One noun calls for all nouns, and so forth. Make sure everything is equal.

> **No:** I didn't realize vampire guts were so **icky, gooey,** and **covered in gunk.**

> **Yes:** I didn't realize vampire guts were so **icky, gooey,** and **gunky.**

The same is true for lists that have phrases. All your phrases should be worded in the same manner.

> **No:** To get the vampire intestines off my jeans, I **scrubbed** *off the chunky bits*, **soaked** *them in hot water*, and **I went and found** *some Guts-Be-Gone to apply*.

> **Yes:** To get the vampire intestines off my jeans, I **scrubbed** *off the chunky bits*, **soaked** *them in hot water*, and **applied** *some Guts-Be-Gone*.

Even little words like **a, an,** or **the** can knock your list off kilter.

> **No: The** zombies, **the** werewolves, vampires, and ghouls like to snack on people.

> **Yes: The** zombies, **the** werewolves, **the** vampires, and **the** ghouls like to snack on people.

> **Yes:** Zombies, werewolves, vampires, and ghouls like to snack on people.

You can also start your list with just one **a, an,** or **the** and leave it at that, but don't just randomly throw them into your list.

> **No:** Personally, I don't see why they can't just snack on **an** apple, orange, or **a** banana like everyone else.

> **Yes:** Personally, I don't see why they can't just snack on **an** apple, **an** orange, or **a** banana like everyone else.

> **Yes:** Personally, I don't see why they can't just snack on **an** apple, orange, or banana like everyone else.

Advanced parallels. Want to take your writing to the next level? Check to make sure your whole sentence is balanced. It's a lot trickier than it sounds, but if you learn to spot these kinds of mistakes, your sentences will improve dramatically.

Check this out:

> **No:** That vampire hunter was **wise** and **a hottie.**

Well, **wise** is an adjective and **hottie** is a noun, so this isn't parallel. It should be:

Yes: That vampire hunter was **wise** and **hot.** *(two adjectives)*

Yes: That vampire hunter was **a sage** and **a hottie.** *(two nouns)*

Here's a tougher one:

No: She used to avoid garlic, but now **garlic is eaten** by her all the time.

Ah, what a sneaky little sentence. The problem here is that first I talk about what she's doing, but then mid-sentence I switch to talking about the garlic. As a result, I also switch from active to passive verbs. The poor sentence is unbalanced and awkward. It should be:

Yes: She used to avoid garlic, but now **she eats** garlic all the time.
*(In both halves of the sentence, **she** is the subject. Also, the verbs are both active.)*

Yes: Garlic was something she used to avoid, but now **garlic is** something she eats all the time.
*(In both halves of the sentence, **garlic** is the subject. Also, the verbs are both passive.)*

When it comes to balancing a sentence, the very least you should do is make sure that your lists are parallel. But keep working on the more advanced ways to make your sentences parallel, and before you know it, your sentences will be beautifully symmetrical.

— 22 —

This above all: to the apostrophe be true. The rules it must follow are practiced by few

O h man, the poor abused apostrophe! Look, I get the urge just to shove the little suckers in willy-nilly. But honestly, there's no need for that. Once you get the hang of the basic apostrophe rules, you'll find that apostrophes can be very useful. Let's just chat about the commonly confused stuff, and anytime you like you can check back here if you need a hand.

Contractions. When you form a contraction, you use an apostrophe. Some examples:

Contraction	Example
cannot = can't	I cannot do that. = I can't do that.
do not = don't	I do not want to. = I don't want to.

112

you are = you're	You are right. = You're right.
let us = let's	Let us not fight. = Let's not fight.
it is = it's	It is good. = It's good.
will not = won't	She will not. = She won't.
would not = wouldn't	He would not go. = He wouldn't go.

(People get confused by its-it's and your-you're. See Thing 36 for more info on how to tell these guys apart.)

Missing Letters and Numbers. If you're going to leave a letter or a number out, slap in an apostrophe to hold its place.

> slamming party = slammin' party
> 2009 = '09

Possessives. Here's where the fun really starts. We humans are possessive beings. From the time we're very small, one concept quickly dominates our wee brains: *mine!* Well, if you want to show what belongs to whom, you should make friends with the apostrophe.

113

No apostrophe needed. I'll start with some happy news. Sometimes you don't have to use an apostrophe at all! Possessive pronouns are already possessive on their own. They don't need any help, so just relax. There's no extra *s* and no apostrophe needed.

> **No:** his' chair
> **Yes:** his chair
>
> **No:** your's coffee mug
> **Yes:** your coffee mug
>
> **No:** That printer is our's.
> **Yes:** That printer is ours.

Here's a list of the **possessive pronouns** for your reference:

her-hers
its
our-ours
your-yours

his
my-mine
their-theirs
whose

Singular Possessive. If it's a singular noun, stick the apostrophe in front of the *s*.

> the new guy's desk = There's one new guy, and that desk belongs to him.
>
> Joan's stapler = That stapler belongs to Joan.

And now for the bit that messes everyone up: What if your singular noun already ends in *s?* Good news: it's the same rule! Just add your *'s* and move on.

> the address's location = The location belongs to that address.
>
> Mr. Jones's rolodex = The rolodex belongs to Mr. Jones.

Let's try some apostrophe practice with what we've learned so far, shall we?

No:
Thats Joans' stapler. Seriously, man, don't touch that. Its her's. Your going to lose a limb if you mess with Joans's stapler. She's had that thing since the 80's and she doesn't like anyone else touching it.

Actually, you shouldn't touch Mr. Jones'
rolodex, either. If you want to figure out
that address' location, look it up on the
Internet.

Let's take these mistakes in order:

thats: should be *that's* because it's a contraction for "that is."
Joans': should be *Joan's* stapler, because the stapler belongs to one Joan, not many Joans.
its: should be *it's* because this is a contraction for "it is."
her's: should be *hers* because *hers* is a possessive pronoun, and therefore doesn't need an apostrophe.
your: should be *you're* because it's a contraction for "you are."
Joans's: should be *Joan's* because there is just one Joan and the stapler is hers.
80's: while you could argue for *'s* as a matter of style, this is still missing the apostrophe before the 8; it should be *'80s* or *'80's* (better yet, print year dates in full: *1980s*).
Mr. Jones': should be *Mr. Jones's* because there's only one Mr. Jones and the rolodex belongs to him.
address': should be *address's* because there's only one address belonging to that location.

Much better:

That's Joan's stapler. Seriously, man, don't touch that. It's hers. You're going to lose a limb if you mess with Joan's stapler. She's had that thing since the '80s and she doesn't like anyone else touching it.

Actually, you shouldn't touch Mr. Jones's rolodex, either. If you want to figure out that address's location, look it up on the Internet.

Plural Possessive. Plural possessives can look really awkward, so it makes sense that they cause so much confusion. Plural possessives are also harder to cope with because there are two parts to them.

Part One: My word is plural but it does not end in an *s.* Well, that's the easy part, people! Just add an 's and go about your business.

> women's bathroom = the bathroom that's for the women
>
> mice's hiding spot = the spot where the mice hide

> people's supplies = the supplies that
> belong to the people

And now for the **other bit** that messes everyone up:

Part Two: My word is plural and ends in an *s*. Okay, just
add an apostrophe. Ta-dah! That's it. Stop there. Pause and
look at the beautiful simplicity of your work. Then, move on.
Whatever you do, do not add an *'s*.

Personally, this is the rule that taxes what's left of my brain.
I usually go back to double-check to make sure I haven't
messed this up.

> The new workers' orientations went
> smoothly. = There were multiple new
> workers and their orientations went well.
>
> The Joneses' car wheezed as it drove
> by. = The car that belongs to multiple
> members of the Jones family was
> making a bad noise.
>
> The women attacked their dresses'
> stains. = There were many women
> wearing many different dresses, which
> had stains.

And on an odd note: Scissors is a weird word. It's both singular and plural. We treat it as a plural, though, so stick that apostrophe after the *s.*

> the scissors' handle = the handle of the scissors

Let's try some more possessives practice, shall we?

No:
We thought that all of the new worker's orientations were very educational. Apparently, someone forgot to talk about office decorum. Their first day on the job, three of the new guy's took chairs that weren't theirs'—they stole them from other peoples' desks. Then another new guy apparently thought its funny when you shake up a can of cola and it explodes all over the place. Of course, it wasn't funny at all when he wound up soaking the nearby womens' dresses. So then the women were fuming that they're dresses' were stained, and there was a stampede for the ladie's bathroom. We made the new guys clean up the mess, but there's probably still some sticky cola residue, much to the

miceses' delight. Fortunately, we got things mostly straightened out before we heard the Joneses car, signaling our boss' return from lunch.

Let's take these mistakes in order:

worker's: should be *workers'* because there were multiple workers and it was their orientation.

guy's: should be *guys* because this isn't possessive.

theirs': should be *theirs* because *theirs* is a possessive pronoun, and therefore doesn't need you to add an *s* or an apostrophe.

peoples': should be *people's.* Since this is a plural, possessive word that doesn't end in *s,* you just add an *'s* to show that the desks belong to them.

its: should be *it's* because this is a contraction for "it is."

womens': should be *women's.* Since this is a plural, possessive word that doesn't end in *s,* you just add an *'s* to show that the dresses belong to them.

they're: should be *their,* which is a possessive pronoun meaning "belonging to them"; *they're* stands for "they are," which doesn't make sense in this context.

dresses': should be *dresses* because this word is not possessive, it's just plain old plural.

ladie's: should be *ladies'* because there is more than one lady and the bathroom belongs to them.

miceses': should be *mice's* because *miceses* isn't a word; the plural of *mouse* is *mice* and then you add the *'s* to show that the delight belongs to them.

Joneses: should be *Joneses'* because there's more than one Jones and the car belongs to them.

boss': should be *boss's* because there's only one boss and it's his return.

> **Much better:**
> We thought that all of the new workers' orientations were very educational. Apparently, someone forgot to talk about office decorum. Their first day on the job, three of the new guys took chairs that weren't theirs—they stole them from other people's desks. Then another new guy apparently thought it's funny when you shake up a can of cola and it explodes all over the place. Of course, it wasn't funny at all when he wound up soaking the nearby women's dresses. So then the women were fuming that their dresses were stained, and there was a stampede for the ladies' bathroom. We made the new guys clean up the mess, but there's probably still some sticky

cola residue, much to the mice's delight. Fortunately, we got things mostly straightened out before we heard the Joneses' car, signaling our boss's return from lunch.

A matter of style. Some apostrophe rules are flexible. Numbers and letters are perfect examples. Some people like to use apostrophes with them, others don't. Don't let these wishy-washy rules make you nuts. If you're using a style guide, follow the guide. Otherwise, just decide for yourself whether you prefer an apostrophe, and then be consistent about it.

The one must-have rule. There is one important rule to follow with letters. Use apostrophes with letters when you need them for clarity. Let's say I'm talking about the letters *i* and *a*. Look what happens when I write them without the apostrophe:

> **No:** is and as
> **Yes:** *i*'s and *a*'s

If I don't use the apostrophe, they look like the words *is* and *as,* when I'm trying to talk about the letters *i* and *a*. That's confusing, so add the apostrophe for clarity.

Overall, apostrophes are supposed to be a tool to help you. Remember, the number-one goal of any piece of writing is to communicate effectively. With that in mind, use apostrophes to make what you're saying clear.

Seriously, people . . .

Its' is not a word. I know y'all get confused by the word *its*. Let me help you by taking one possible spelling off the table. There is no such thing as *its'*. You only have to decide between *its* and *it's*.

> **No:** I'm so glad its' over.
>
> **Yes:** I'm so glad it's over.
>
> **No:** I hope the Human Resources Department gets its' act together and organizes its' orientations.
>
> **Yes:** I hope the Human Resources Department gets its act together and organizes its orientations.

— 23 —

Colons would make excellent pimps. Their job is to point you in a specific direction and to get you to notice their wares

I find colons lovely in their simplicity. No matter how you use a colon, its main function is to say "Yoo-hoo" and get you to look over, pause, and pay attention.

Despite their usefulness, colons don't get a lot of work these days. There seems to be confusion over how to use them. Use colons to let your reader know there's a list, explanation, or long quotation coming up.

List. The most common way to use a colon is with a list. Since not all lists have colons, you might be wondering why you'd need to use colons at all. If you have a complete sentence before your list, then use a colon. If not, then you don't need it.

> **Colon:** When beaming down to a new planet, your survival gear should include three things: five easy-swallow meal

capsules, an instant housing unit, and some sunscreen.

(In this example, "When beaming down to a new planet, your survival gear should include three things" forms a complete sentence, so I used a colon before my list.)

No colon: When beaming down to a new planet, your survival gear should include five easy-swallow meal capsules, an instant housing unit, and some sunscreen.

(I've changed the example so that "When beaming down to a new planet, your survival gear should include" no longer forms a complete sentence. Thus, I don't need a colon before my list.)

Here's a little test you can perform. Try replacing the colon with the word **namely.** If the sentence still makes sense, then keep your colon. If it doesn't, the colon isn't needed.

Please note that you do *not* capitalize the items in a list when they come after a colon, unless the word would normally be capitalized.

No: Female cadets wear these items: **B**lack **B**oots, **G**ray **T**ights, and **S**hort **D**resses.

Still no: Female cadets wear these items: **B**lack boots, **G**ray tights, and **S**hort dresses.

Yes: Female cadets wear these items: **b**lack boots, **g**ray tights, and **s**hort dresses.

Yes: Female cadets wear these items: **M**ercury boots, **g**ray tights, and **s**hort dresses.

Explanation. A bit trickier usage of the colon comes when you use it in place of a semicolon. Both punctuation marks can glue two sentences together, but you use a colon when you want to say, "Hey, look at the explanation that's coming next." Choose a colon over a semicolon when you want to place the emphasis on the second sentence. Check out this example:

> One thing is for sure: somehow the dude in the red shirt always gets shot.

I'm thinking that if you're going down to the alien planet, then the second part of this sentence should indeed be emphasized with a colon. It's going to be important to you if you want to stay alive. Also, the second part provides an explanation about the first part. So, in this case, a colon is preferable to a semicolon.

To cap or not to cap? Look at the same example again:

> One thing is for sure: **somehow** the
> dude in the red shirt always gets shot.

How come the *s* in **somehow** isn't capitalized? It's a complete sentence, after all. We're back to arguing about style again. Some grammar books will tell you that you must capitalize a complete sentence if it comes after the colon. Others will tell you not to. You have to make up your own mind, then be consistent about it. Or, if you're using a style guide, you have to do what they tell you. I'm using the *Chicago Manual of Style* to write this book, and it says no capital after the colon, so that's how I'm handling it.

Long Quotation. If you have a long quotation, you can use a colon to introduce it. As usual, the colon tells your reader, "Hey, look at this."

With a long quotation, all you need is the colon. You

don't even need to use quotation marks. Just set the quotation in a paragraph by itself.

> In *The Restaurant at the End of the Universe,* Douglas Adams wrote:
>
> There is a theory which states that if ever anyone discovers exactly what the Universe is for and why it is here, it will instantly disappear and be replaced by something even more bizarre and inexplicable. There is another which states that this has already happened.
>
> ~*Douglas Adams,* The Restaurant at the End of the Universe *(New York: Wings Books, 1989)*

You won't use colons all that often in your writing. But when you want to say, "Yo! Pay attention to what comes next!" the colon is your go-to guy.

Seriously, people . . .

These days, lists often involve bullet points. I regret to inform you that how you format your list of bullets is really a matter of style. You can capitalize each bullet—or not. You can put a period at the end of each bullet—or not.

But seriously, whatever bullet format you choose, *pick one style and stick with it.* If you're going to capitalize one bullet, then capitalize them all. If you want to add a period to one, then you're going to have to make sure the others match.

For the Love of Pete, No:

If you want to survive your mission:
1. **D**o not wear a red shirt.
2. **d**o not mock the aliens.
3. **d**o not wander away from the landing party
4. **D**o not poke anything with a stick

As you can see, in this bulleted list capitals and periods are used at random. Please, oh please, do not do this. It's distracting and sloppy. If your writing looks as if you didn't make any kind of effort when you wrote it, why should your reader go to the effort of reading it?

This is okay:

(consistently uses caps and periods)

If you want to survive your mission:
1. Do not wear a red shirt.
2. Do not mock the aliens.
3. Do not wander away from the landing party.
4. Do not poke anything with a stick.

This is okay, too:

(consistently omits caps and periods)

Survive your mission by:
1. not wearing a red shirt
2. not mocking the aliens
3. not wandering away from the landing party
4. not poking anything with a stick

This is also okay:

(consistently omits caps, uses periods)

Survive your mission by:
1. not wearing a red shirt.
2. not mocking the aliens.
3. not wandering away from the landing party.
4. not poking anything with a stick.

If you have more than one bulleted list in your memo, paper, report, or email, then please format them all the same. Be consistently consistent.

Seriously, people . . .

If you're writing a formal letter or a formal business email, please use a colon with your salutation. It's not only proper, it's polite.

> **No:** Dear Mr. Givemeajob,
> **No:** Dear Mr. Givemeajob
> **Yes:** Dear Mr. Givemeajob:

$-24-$

Commas are kind of like politicians. There are usually too many of them and they're often not where they should be

There are no two ways about it: commas are wily little buggers. Want to know the ugly truth? When it comes to commas, how you use them is largely a matter of style. That means that unlike other grammar rules, many comma rules seem to have a sort of wishy-washiness that can make you want to bang your head on a stick.

I do, however, have good news! I'm not going to torment you with every permutation of every possible comma rule out there. Seriously, I won't even try to cover all the comma rules. We're only going to talk about the things that tend to trip us up the most.

Go for clarity! Remember that you want your reader to be able to understand whatever you've written. So the most important thing is to use your commas to provide clarity. If that means you have to add or subtract a comma here and there, then do it.

Use a comma with your conjunction when you're gluing two sentences together. The comma and conjunction combo will help you to avoid a comma splice error. *(To learn about comma splice errors, see Thing 18.)*

> **No:** We were standing in line at the store **and** I was reading the *Tattletale Tabloid.*
>
> **Yes:** We were standing in line at the store**, and** I was reading the *Tattletale Tabloid.*
>
> **No:** Petunia had been sitting quietly in the cart**,** suddenly she was gone.
>
> **Yes:** Petunia had been sitting quietly in the cart**, but** suddenly she was gone.

Use a comma to set off a long opening phrase or clause. Good writers vary their sentence structures. Occasionally, you'll want to start a sentence with a clause or phrase that depends on the remainder of the sentence to complete its thought. When you do, set off that clause with a comma.

> **No:** When I looked up Petunia was riding down the conveyor belt.
>
> **Yes:** When I looked up**,** Petunia was riding down the conveyor belt.

No: As I watched the clerk scanned
Petunia and put her in a bag.

Yes: As I watched, the clerk scanned
Petunia and put her in a bag.

Please note: there is disagreement on when to use a comma after an opening phrase. A safe bet is that if the phrase is longer than three words, you need a comma for clarity. If it's three words or fewer, then it's usually a matter of style. The second example above is an exception, because the three-word phrase is confusing without the comma.

Here is another exception: Use a comma after transitional words and phrases, like **therefore, however, for example, for instance,** and so forth.

Afterward, I wondered at how calm I
remained.

For instance, it didn't occur to me to
panic.

Use a comma to set off interrupters and asides. Asides and interrupters are any little comments that don't have to do with the main meaning of the sentence.

Well, **as you can imagine,** I didn't know what to do at first.

I quickly recovered, **however,** and made a lunge for my Petunia-in-a-bag.

Use a comma to set off nonessential information or extra description. Got an extra detail you want to include, even though it's not part of the main meaning of your sentence? Set it off with commas.

I took a giant leap, **floating gracefully through the air,** as I reached out for the bag.
(We don't need "floating gracefully through the air" to get the meaning of the sentence, so it's set off with commas.)

Unfortunately, I missed the bag but grabbed the clerk's shirt, **which was a deplorable shade of green.**
(We don't need "which was a deplorable shade of green" to get the meaning of the sentence, thus the comma. For more information on when to use that, who, or which, see Thing 9.)

Topher, **the clerk,** was so busy glaring at me that he didn't see what was coming next.

("The clerk" is an appositive, renaming Topher, so it gets set off with commas.)

Use a comma between things in a list. Whether your list consists of single words or longer phrases, you should separate your items clearly.

> While the clerk was turned toward me, Petunia **poked her head out of the bag, looked around, and zeroed in on the clerk.**

(The introductory phrase "while the clerk was turned toward me" gets a comma. Then, there are three phrases in a list, so they are set off with commas, too.)

> Petunia didn't **growl, bark,** or **whine.**

(The commas separate the things in this list.)

> However, the clerk **howled, yelped, and shouted** when Petunia leaned over and bit the baggy butt of his jeans.

(The transitional word "however" gets a comma, as do the things in the list.)

An exception: If the items in your list already have commas, separate the items with semicolons. *(For more on semicolons, see Thing 30.)*

> While the clerk flailed about, a pickle jar smashed, spewing pickle juice everywhere; the eggs fell over, cracking and oozing on the conveyor belt; and the milk carton ripped, dripping milk onto the clerk's shoes.

Remember that using commas is like adding spices to a recipe. Too much or too little will wreck your dish. But used with thought and care, they make everything better.

Seriously, people . . .

Serial commas is the fancy term for putting commas between items in a list. The whole debate about serial commas makes me put my cranky pants on. Depending on what style you follow, you either use a comma before the last thing in the list—or not. I really hate the "no comma before the last thing" style, but some style guides insist on it.

Whether you're following a style guide, or just using your own style, here's what you need to remember:

1. Be consistent. Either use serial commas or don't, but please pick one approach and stick with it in any given piece of writing.

2. Be clear. Sometimes you simply have to use a comma or your list doesn't make sense. In particular, clarity can be an issue if the items in your list are phrases, or if one of the items contains the word **and.**

> **No:** A huge commotion ensued with Petunia refusing to let go, the clerk dancing around and **yelling and** me trying to calm them both down.

> **Yes:** A huge commotion ensued with Petunia refusing to let go, the clerk dancing around and **yelling, and** me trying to calm them both down.

By adding the comma before the **and,** I made the sentence clearer.

As I said before, clarity comes first, so use the comma if you need to. Better yet, adopt a style guide that prescribes using the serial comma.

– 25 –

Dashes aren't just ostentatious hyphens

Did you know that a dash isn't the same thing as a hyphen? Certainly there's a familial resemblance, but they belong to separate clans and live totally separate existences. Chances are that you are overworking your hyphens and underutilizing your dashes.

Let your dash do the heavy lifting! For bigger jobs, like linking thoughts and phrases, use your dash. But for smaller jobs, like linking individual words, stick with the little hyphen. *(For more on hyphens, see Thing 27.)*

Ah, but the plot thickens! Did you know that there are two kinds of dashes? Depending on what you need, you can choose a dash to match your purpose.

The em dash. Of the two dashes, this is the one you really need to know—this is the one you'll use more often. When you hear people refer to "the dash," this is the one they mean.

The em dash looks like this: —
"Em" refers to the length of a size of type, which is expressed in points. Thus, 9-point type would include an em dash 9 points in width. Anytime you see a long dash, it's most likely an em dash.

I have to warn you that em dashes are frowned upon in formal writing, unless it's poetry. In formal writing, if you can use any other kind of punctuation and still get the job done, then go with that.

Want to try your hand at dashing?

- **Use the em dash for an abrupt change in thought.**

The one place where em dashes are really useful, even in formal writing, is when you have an abrupt change or interruption in thought. Use the dash to separate the thoughts.

> Honey, about your outfit—would you put that down and listen, please?

- **Beware too much dashing around!**

If you're writing more informally, you can sometimes get away with using the em dash in place of other punctuation. But let me warn you: the em dash is seductive. Once you start dashing, it's quite easy to get carried away. Just try to keep your dashing about under control, and reserve the em dash for the times when you want to emphasize something.

> Sweetheart, that jacket—with all that plaid—does not match those yellow pants.

(If this was formal writing, I could have used commas here.)

> I have excellent fashion sense—you are so lucky!

(In this case, I could have used a semicolon.)

The en dash. You may never use an en dash at all, but you should know what it is.

> The en dash looks like this: –.
> It's longer than a hyphen, but half the width of an em dash.

You use an en dash to show a range of numbers, including times and dates. Many people just use a hyphen for these things. But, if you can replace the hyphen in the range with the word **to,** then you can also use an en dash. Most people just go with the hyphen and ignore the en dash, and there's a movement afoot to get rid of the en dash altogether.

        1983–1984 (the years 1983 to 1984)
        pages 2–7 (pages 2 to 7)
        9:00–10:00 (nine o'clock to ten o'clock)

Don't get caught using a hyphen when what you really want is a dash. Yes, you want to exercise some restraint with dashes, but don't discount them. You'll miss out on all the fun dashing about!

– 26 –

Your ellipses should look as if you put them there on purpose, not as if your pen sneezed on your page

Y ou know those three dots you see hanging about in sentences? They look like this: . . .

Those are called ellipses. If you see them, it doesn't mean the sentence has the measles, chicken pox, or some other dreadful spotted disease. Ellipses are a type of punctuation.

Ellipses always have three dots. That's *three* dots, people! Not one, not two, and certainly not five.

Sometimes, it looks as if an ellipsis has four dots when it comes at the end of a complete sentence. But that's because there's a period included.

Ellipses tell you when something has been omitted. If you're quoting something and you need to leave part of it out, use ellipses.

Quotation:

> *"Once upon a midnight dreary, while I*
> *pondered, weak and weary,*
> *Over many a quaint and curious*
> *volume of forgotten lore,*
> *While I nodded, nearly napping,*
> *suddenly there came a tapping,*
> *As of some one gently rapping, rapping*
> *at my chamber door."*
>
> ~from "The Raven," Edgar Allan Poe

With ellipses, indicating an omission:

> "Once upon a midnight dreary . . .
> suddenly there came a . . . rapping at
> my chamber door."

Ellipses also tell you when a thought has paused or trailed off. Here, there's a pause in the middle of the sentence.

> Let me see . . . a little oil should stop
> the door from making all that noise.

Here, the thought trails off without finishing.

> "Maybe you dreamed that whole rapping
> at the door thing . . .?" she asked.

For some reason, ellipses seem to get overlooked a lot, but they're really helpful in situations where you have omissions and interruptions.

Seriously, people . . .

It's unethical to change the original meaning of something you're quoting. By leaving out certain bits, it's all too easy to creatively edit someone's original intention. Please don't do this!

We've all heard of cases where an interviewer has twisted the words of an interviewee by omitting relevant information. Unfortunately, it's really easy to manipulate anything quoted by taking out a few words here and there.

Original quotation:

> *The Hitchhikers Guide to the Galaxy*
> has this to say on the subject of flying.

> There is an art, it says, or, rather,
> a knack to flying. The knack lies in
> learning how to throw yourself at the
> ground and miss.
>> ~*Douglas Adams,* Life, the Universe, and
>> Everything *(New York: Wings Books, 1989)*

Unethically edited quotation:

> *The Hitchhikers Guide to the Galaxy* . . .
> on the subject of flying . . . says . . . to
> throw yourself at the ground.

Well, that just sounds painful. Even worse, that's not what Adams was actually saying in his story. We've lost the meaning, not to mention the humor, of the original piece.

Sometimes it's necessary to shorten a quotation. But when you omit words, be careful to maintain the integrity of your source material.

Hyphens are not just young dashes waiting for a growth spurt

The poor little hyphen gets overworked because it often gets confused with the dash. *(For more on dashes, see Thing 25.)*

A hyphen is not a dash! Think of it this way: hyphens are smaller, so they have smaller jobs. Hyphens link words together, while dashes link phrases.

What are some common ways to use a hyphen?

Adjectives before a noun may need a hyphen. After the noun, they don't. (For more on adjectives, see Thing 11.)

> **No:** No wonder she spilled it; she's only **two-years-old.**
>
> **Yes:** No wonder she spilled it; **she's only two years old.**
>
> **Yes:** No wonder she spilled it; **she's a two-year-old child.**

Use a hyphen when your prefix would make your word confusing.

> I had to **re-treat** that stain.

If I don't hyphenate **re-treat,** I wind up with **retreat,** which means "to withdraw or move back." A stain might be so bad we end up retreating from it, but if I hope to eradicate it, I've got "to treat it again." To clarify, you need a hyphen.

Use a hyphen to link numbers, including fractions. (For more on writing numbers, see Thing 33.)

> one-fourth
> forty-two

Spelling. Some words are always hyphenated as part of their spelling.

> mother-in-law
> yoo-hoo
> wishy-washy

For such little guys, hyphens are quite useful. Just follow the rules and you'll be on your way to hyphenating heaven.

– 28 –

Parentheses are not an excuse to forget everything else you know about grammar

Honestly, I don't know what it is about parentheses that makes people toss all their grammar knowledge to the wind. For some reason, when people use parentheses they think that capitalization and punctuation are no longer necessary.

If the parentheses are part of your sentence, you still need a period at the end of the sentence.

> **No:** Enclosed, please find your
> superhero starter kit (inside the box)

The period should go at the end of the sentence, *outside* the parentheses, when the parentheses are part of the sentence.

> **Still no:** Enclosed, please find your
> superhero starter kit. (inside the box)

> **Yes:** Enclosed, please find your superhero starter kit (inside the box)**.**

If the parentheses contain their own separate, complete sentence, treat the sentence the way you normally would. Just because your sentence is inside the parentheses is no excuse not to use a capital letter at the beginning and punctuation at the end.

> **No:** Fighting bad guys is no excuse for a wrinkly cape. (have you ever seen Superman's or Batman's cape after a fight)

> **Yes:** Fighting bad guys is no excuse for a wrinkly cape. (**H**ave you ever seen Superman's or Batman's cape after a fight**?**)

If it's supposed to be capitalized, then capitalize it inside the parentheses, too.

> **No:** Good superheroes keep their footwear shiny at all times (like **w**onder **w**oman's boots).

> **Yes:** Good superheroes keep their footwear shiny at all times (like **W**onder **W**oman's boots).

150

If it's a list, make sure you use commas and keep your items parallel, just as you would with any other list.

> **No:** Your costume (including your spandex tights armored breastplate and cape you can wear in any weather) should always be clean and pressed.

> **Yes:** Your costume (including your spandex tights, armored breastplate, and all-weather cape) should always be clean and pressed.

Your sentence should read correctly even when the parenthetical is removed. Parentheses contain information that interrupts a sentence, like explanations, examples, and asides. The information in parentheses should be an addition to the main meaning of the sentence, so that if you take the parentheses (and their contents) away, the sentence should still be fine on its own.

> **No:** Do not use hot water on (or apply harsh cleaning agents) to your tights.
> *(If you take the parentheses out, the sentence doesn't make sense.)*

> **Yes:** Do not use hot water on (or apply harsh cleaning agents to) your tights.

*(By moving the **to** inside the parentheses, the sentence now make sense if you remove the parentheses.)*

The words inside parentheses give us examples and clarify information. Just because they're inside the parentheses doesn't mean that we should treat them as inferior. They should be treated with the same grammatical respect as the rest of our writing.

Forget putting the lime in the coconut. Just put the period and the comma inside the quotes and we'll all be happy

Okay, people. Say it with me:

"The period and the comma always go *inside* the quotation marks."

Make this your new mantra if you must, but please, oh please, put them inside the quotes. Don't leave them out in the cold. That's just mean.

Why is this so confusing? Because other punctuation has other rules.

*The period and the comma always go **inside** the quotation marks.* To me, this rule can be confusing because often it looks weird when you do it right.

> **No:** If you haven't already read Millay's poem "What Lips My Lips Have Kissed**",**

then I highly recommend you check it out.

Yes: If you haven't already read Millay's poem "What Lips My Lips Have Kissed**,"** then I highly recommend you check it out.

No: Although Del Amitri's song "Roll to Me" was the hit, her favorite song on the album was "Here and Now**".**

Yes: Although Del Amitri's song "Roll to Me" was the hit, her favorite song on the album was "Here and Now**."**

Check out how it looks with dialogue.

No: "Yes, I like to read poetry**",** he said.

Yes: "Yes, I like to read poetry**,"** he said.

No: "I find it helps with my songwriting**".**

Yes: "I find it helps with my songwriting**."**

154

*Colons and semicolons go **outside** the quotation marks.* As if using colons and semicolons wasn't tricky enough!

> **No:** He says that Pop Princess's song is an "earworm**:"** it gets stuck in your head and won't leave.

> **Yes:** He says that Pop Princess's song is an "earworm"**:** it gets stuck in your head and won't leave.

> **No:** I love Dylan's "Things Have Changed**;"** that song proves his music is still rockin' and relevant.

> **Yes:** I love Dylan's "Things Have Changed"**;** that song proves his music is still rockin' and relevant.

*Dashes, exclamation points, and question marks **can go either way.*** Really, I wish this rule applied to everything, because it just seems logical.

If the dash, exclamation point, or question mark applies to the *entire sentence* (not to just what's inside the quotes), it goes *outside* the quotation marks.

> **No:** Have you ever heard Rhett Miller's song "I Need to Know Where I Stand**?"**

Yes: Have you ever heard Rhett Miller's song "I Need to Know Where I Stand"**?**

No: I can't believe I just listened to a polka version of "Enter the Sandman**!"**

Yes: I can't believe I just listened to a polka version of "Enter the Sandman"**!**

No: I heard clapping after I finished reciting Auden's "Funeral Blues—" I assumed it was for me.

Yes: I heard clapping after I finished reciting Auden's "Funeral Blues"—I assumed it was for me.

But if the dash, exclamation point, or question mark applies *only to what's inside the quotes,* it goes *inside* the quotation marks.

No: In school, he'd studied Kiplings's poem "If"— and still remembered it after all these years.

Yes: In school, he'd studied Kiplings's poem "If—" and still remembered it after all these years.

(The dash is part of the title of the poem.)

No: The slogan on the poster screamed "Rock Hard**"!** in huge orange letters.

Yes: The slogan on the poster screamed "Rock Hard**!"** in huge orange letters.

(The exclamation point is part of the slogan.)

No: He wanted to write something with a rockin' beat, like "Would I Lie to You**"?** by the Eurythmics.

Yes: He wanted to write something with a rockin' beat, like "Would I Lie to You**?"** by the Eurythmics.

(The question mark is part of the title of the song.)

Check out how it looks with dialogue.

No: "How can that possibly be one of your top ten favorite songs**"?** she asked.

Yes: "How can that possibly be one of your top ten favorite songs**?"** she asked.

No: "Have you heard the**"—** he said.

Yes: "Have you heard the**—"** he said.

No: "Yeah, I've heard the whole thing, and I still think it bites**"!** she said.

Yes: "Yeah, I've heard the whole thing, and I still think it bites**!**" she said.

Most quotation marks have two curls, not one.

No: 'I know you really love that song,' she said.

Yes: "I know you really love that song," she said.

You only use a single curl when you're quoting within a quotation. Otherwise, a single curl is really an apostrophe, and not a quotation mark at all.

No: "But every time I hear the lyrics "your buns are hotter than Aunt Polly's Sunday rolls" I can't take the song seriously," she said.

Yes: "But every time I hear the lyrics 'your buns are hotter than Aunt Polly's Sunday rolls' I can't take the song seriously," she said.

If you don't like the quotation rules, I don't blame you. They can look really wonky. But if you don't follow them, then your writing can be really unclear and hard to read. Quotation errors look really horrible and just ruin your writing.

Seriously, people . . .

If you're quoting something, you are supposed to quote it *exactly* as is. This means that if your quotation comes with mistakes, you're stuck keeping the mistakes. That's no good, because you don't want it to look as if you're the one who made the mistake. Fortunately, we have a way around this!

If you are quoting something with grammatical errors, spelling issues, and so on, put the term [*sic*] after it (in italics and square brackets, just like that). [*Sic*] basically means "Dude, I didn't mess this up—it came this way!"

All that glitters ain't [*sic*] gold.

− 30 −

Semicolons are like the cowboys of punctuation. Call on them when you need something strong to corral your sentence

Need a little extra muscle for your sentence? Bring in the semicolon. Granted, a semicolon looks like a colon that's having a bad hair day, but don't let the goofy appearance fool you. When other punctuation isn't strong enough to get the job done, the semicolon comes to the rescue.

Use a semicolon to link two independent thoughts or sentences. Semicolons can glue two sentences together all by themselves. They don't need extra conjunctions or transition words; they're fine on their own.

> **No:** I asked for *The Tick* for my birthday, I guess my mom doesn't know it's a TV show, because I got an ant farm instead.

> **Yes:** I asked for *The Tick* for my birthday; I guess my mom doesn't know it's a TV show, because I got an ant farm instead.

(The "No" sentence is an example of a comma splice error. For more on fixing this kind of error, see Thing 18.)

Use semicolons to rescue a loaded list. Semicolons are also dead useful when you have a list that's lousy with commas. The semicolons will wade right in there and sort that list out. If the items in your list are really long or include commas, use semicolons to separate the items.

No: On my wish list, I have a TARDIS, from London, England, which makes that awesome whirring noise, a Cylon Raider, with a glowing eye, which makes that awesome Cylon noise, and an Arthur Dent action figure, which makes no noise, but comes with a towel!

Yes: On my wish list, I have a TARDIS, from London, England, which makes that awesome whirring noise; a Cylon Raider, with a glowing eye, which makes that awesome Cylon noise; and an Arthur Dent action figure, which makes no noise, but comes with a towel!

Do not capitalize the letter that comes after the semicolon, unless it would normally be capitalized. Whether you're using your semicolon to separate a list or to glue two sentences together, no extra capital letters are needed.

No: For my birthday, we went shopping and bought some books, written by Terry Brooks and Patricia Briggs; **S**ome comic books, written by Joss Whedon; **A**nd some chocolate, made by Godiva.

Yes: For my birthday, we went shopping and bought some books, written by Terry Brooks and Patricia Briggs; **s**ome comic books, written by Joss Whedon; **a**nd some chocolate, made by Godiva.

No: After I read *The Dark Tower* novels, I received the comic books as a gift; **T**hey're incredibly good.

Yes: After I read *The Dark Tower* novels, I received the comic books as a gift; **t**hey're incredibly good.

I know that semicolons look kinda funny—sort of like the love child of a colon and a comma—but they're really very useful. If you're not using them in your writing, you're missing out.

~ 31 ~

Titles don't like running around naked in public any more than I do

Titles of things get lonely. Book titles, TV titles, song titles—you name it. They need a little extra attention, either in the form of quotation marks or italics.

In contrast, titles of people don't need any extra stuff. They're already attached to people, so they're not lonely.

Titles of short works go in quotes. I think of short works like small children: they like lots of hugs. Keep them hugged by quotation marks and they'll be happy. By short works I mean stuff like articles, poems, songs, short stories, chapters of books, and individual episodes of TV shows.

- article:
    The article "Could Jupiter Moon Harbor Fish-Size Life?" inspired the teacher to have students design alien fish for their art projects.
- book chapter (and book title):

> Tomorrow in class, we're reading "Louis," the fifth chapter of *The Trumpet of the Swan.*

- TV episode (and TV show):
  > Every time I watch the "Victoria's Secret" episodes of *Due South* my heart breaks all over again.

- poem:
  > In her poem "When Death Comes," Mary Oliver says, "When it's over, I want to say: all my life I was a bride married to amazement."

- song:
  > Jude Cole has written lots of great songs, but "Worlds Apart" is one of my favorites.

- short story:
  > He liked Harlan Ellison's "'Repent Harlequin!' Said the Ticktockman" so much that he bought copies of the short story for all his friends.

(Note the quote within a quote in the short story title. That's because part of the title is already inside quotation marks, so to properly punctuate the quote and the title, I used the quote-within-a-quote rule. For more on using quotation marks, see Thing 29.)

Titles of long works are generally italicized. To do that, *generally* you want to put the title in italics. I say *generally* because some style guides still prefer you to underline. But these days, underlining is often confused with hyperlinking, so italicizing has taken precedence.

By long works, I mean stuff like books, magazines, movies, paintings, plays, really long poems, and TV shows.

- book:

   She took her niece to Boston Public Garden where they sat on the grass and read Robert McCloskey's *Make Way for Ducklings*.

- magazine:

   Whom do you think *Time* will pick as the Person of the Year?

- movie:

   It took over two decades for *The Watchmen* to finally be made into a movie, but the wait was worth it.

- painting:

   She wasn't a huge fan of Monet until she saw *Tempête, côtes de Belle-Ile* at the Musée d'Orsay in Paris.

- play:

   Although he's known for his work in film and TV, Alan Ball also wrote a great play called *Five Women Wearing the Same Dress*.

- really long poem:
  Somehow, we avoided having to read *The Iliad* or *The Odyssey* in high school.
- TV show (and episode):
  If you've never seen the episode of *Buffy the Vampire Slayer* called "Hush," then you're really missing out!

Giving your titles a bit of extra attention really pays off. Writing with correctly and consistently formatted titles looks polished and professional.

— 32 —

Unless you're e. e. cummings, capital letters are necessary

Come on, 'fess up. You've written IMs, texts, and even emails without any capital letters, haven't you? I sure have. It's way easier to write using all lowercase letters. I mean, you have to stretch all the way over to the shift key to make a capital. Why strain your pinky?

I've got no problems with lowercase love for IMs and texts. I can even live with it when we're talking about really informal emails. But otherwise, we need capital letters.

As I've said before, the most important thing in writing is clarity. Your reader needs to be able to understand what you're saying. If you want to be clear, you're going to need some capital letters in whatever you're writing.

Of course, using capitals means overcoming capitalization confusion. People mostly know the main rules, like starting a sentence with a capital, capitalizing "I," and capitalizing proper nouns. But there are a few places where people tend to get stuck.

Directions. Capitalize regions but not directions. (I can never remember this one, for some reason, and I always have to check and make sure I'm doing it right.)

> Examples of regions: the Southwest, Northern California, New England
>
> Examples of directions: north, south, east, west

>> **No:** She told us to go **South,** but we went **North** instead.
>>
>> **Yes:** She told us to go **south,** but we went **north** instead.
>
> *(In this example, we're talking about a direction, so no capital letters are used.)*

>> **No:** We were looking forward to visiting Gondor in the **south,** but Rohan turned out to be nice, too.
>>
>> **Yes:** We were looking forward to visiting Gondor in the **South,** but Rohan turned out to be nice, too.
>
> *(Because the South is a geographical region, it gets a capital letter.)*

People's titles. Capitalize a person's title when it comes *before* the name.

No: Yesterday, **president** Aragorn made a speech from the White Tower.

Yes: Yesterday, **President** Aragorn made a speech from the White Tower.

Do *not* capitalize a person's title if it comes *after* the name.

No: Aragorn announced that Treebeard, **Secretary of Forestry,** has instituted a ban on clear-cutting.

Yes: Aragorn announced that Treebeard, **secretary of forestry,** has instituted a ban on clear-cutting.

Capitalize a person's title if you're using it in place of the person's name.

No: We're so glad you stopped by, **steward.**

Yes: We're so glad you stopped by, **Steward.**

Letter and email closings. Capitalize only the first word.

No: Sincerely Yours,

> **Yes:** Sincerely yours,
>
> **No:** Your Best Friend Forever,
>
> **Yes:** Your best friend forever,

Course titles and school subjects. Do not capitalize general course names, but do capitalize specific course titles.

> **No:** What did you study in **Geography** last fall? We're taking **geography 201: the Shire** this semester.
>
> **Yes:** What did you study in **geography** last fall? We're taking **Geography 201: the Shire** this semester.

Exception: Capitalize the general course name if it is a language that would normally be capitalized because it's a proper noun.

> **No:** We studied several of the tree languages in addition to **english.**
>
> **Yes:** We studied several of the tree languages in addition to **English.**

Seasons. Don't capitalize the seasons.

Seasons: winter, spring, summer, fall

> **No:** While Lothlorien is glorious any time of year, **Spring** is a particularly lovely time to visit.

> **Yes:** While Lothlorien is glorious any time of year, **spring** is a particularly lovely time to visit.

Interrupted dialogue. Sometimes dialogue is broken up with interruptions. If the same sentence continues after the interruption, then the second part of the sentence doesn't need a capital. Think of it this way: it's still the same sentence. Since you're not starting a new sentence, you don't need a capital letter.

> **No:** "Since we're heading north," she said, "**W**e might as well stop in at Fangorn and see the Ents."

> **Yes:** "Since we're heading north," she said, "**w**e might as well stop in at Fangorn and see the Ents."

(In this example, the same sentence is continuing on after the "she said" in the middle, so you don't need a capital to start the second

half. Notice there's a comma after "she said"
letting you know the sentence hasn't ended.)

However, if your sentence ends, and a new sentence starts, then you use a capital.

> **No:** "I do love the Ents," he said.
> "**m**aybe Quickbeam will be around."

> **Yes:** "I do love the Ents," he said.
> "**M**aybe Quickbeam will be around."
> *(Note the period after the "he said," letting you*
> *know that the sentence has ended. Since you're*
> *starting a new sentence, you need a capital.)*

I honestly don't expect you to memorize every capitalization rule out there. But don't let capitalization confusion muck up your writing. If you're feeling unsure, just take a few seconds to double-check the rules. Then you don't have to chicken out and use lowercase laziness.

— 33 —

The numbers went to the trouble of coming over to play with your words; you should treat them fairly

It seems as though numbers should be reserved for math, and words should be reserved for writing. Of course, it's never that simple. Often you need numbers for writing, too.

Don't start a sentence with a numeral. If your sentence begins with a number, either write out the number or reword the sentence.

> **No:** 200 balloons arrived for the party.
>
> **Yes:** Two hundred balloons arrived for the party.
>
> **Yes:** I ordered 200 balloons, which arrived the day of the party.
>
> **No:** ¾ of the balloons were tied to the table with the cake on it.
>
> **Yes:** Three-quarters of the balloons were tied to the table with the cake on it.

Yes: The table with the cake on it had ¾ of the balloons tied to it.

Use hyphens when you write out compound numbers from twenty-one to ninety-nine.

No: The cake was supposed to feed all **twenty five** of our guests.

Yes: The cake was supposed to feed all **twenty-five** of our guests.

Use numerals for the exact time. Instead of trying to write out a specific time, just stick with numerals.

No: It was **seven minutes past two o'clock in the afternoon** when the table started to float off the ground, taking the cake with it.

Yes: It was **2:07 p.m.** when the table started to float off the ground, taking the cake with it.

Write out noon and midnight.

No: The cake had been delivered at **12:00 p.m.**

Yes: The cake had been delivered at **noon.**

No: The table with the cake didn't come back down until **12:00 a.m.**

Yes: The table with the cake didn't come back down until **midnight.**

General usage: word or numeral? Other than these rules, when else should you use a word instead of a numeral? Basically, you just want to be consistent. Some rules say write out **one** through **nine,** others say to write out **one** through **ninety-nine** or **one hundred.** Whichever way you go, just stick with it.

Using numerals instead of letters definitely has some advantages. Looking at numerals can be much easier to understand than trying to read a number that's been spelled out. Writing numerals is also often faster than writing letters. Whatever number formatting you choose, follow the rules and be consistent.

— 34 —

Rely on cruise control to drive your car, and you're an accident waiting to happen. Rely on spell check to edit your writing, and you'll crash and burn just as surely

S pell check is a fair-weather friend. Sure, it's fabulous at finding some of the spelling mistakes that you missed. But it won't find them all.

Don't get me wrong. You should absolutely run spell check before you send off something you've written, particularly if it's a business email, a report, or some other type of formal writing.

But please, oh please, don't rely solely on spell check.

As a writing tutor, spell check was the bane of my existence for two reasons. First, when my students got into situations where they couldn't use spell check, they were misspelling even simple words. This was a disaster when it came to things like taking tests and filling out job applications. Second, instead of checking over their own writing carefully, the students assumed spell check would take care of everything. The results were not pretty.

Lately, I've noticed the same thing happening at work.

More and more, people are relying entirely on spell check. As a result, they're turning in work with huge mistakes.

There are several different things that spell check will miss.

If you leave out a word or accidentally switch the order of your words, spell check won't catch it. Check it out:

> Mr. Smith:
>
> Regarding your question, of course I'd **like chat.** When **you do** want to meet?

This should be:

> Mr. Smith:
>
> Regarding your question, of course I'd like **to** chat. When **do you** want to meet?

These are the kinds of mistakes it's easy to make if you're typing quickly. But they're just as easy to correct if you take the time to do a quick once-over in addition to running spell check. Send it like this and your writing looks sloppy, as if you were too lazy to edit even a simple email. Ouch.

But wait! The fun doesn't stop there!

If you add or drop a letter, creating a word you didn't intend, spell check won't catch it if the new word is spelled correctly. Check it out:

> Dear Potential Employer:
> I **aim** writing in response to your **and.**

Well, you can forget about getting that job. It should read:

> I **am** writing in response to your **ad.**

The chaos is not reserved just for business writing. Those slipups can mess up your personal correspondence something wicked. Mistakes can change the tone and intent of what you're trying to say.

Suppose you send this email:

> Hey,
>
> I'm back home. Wow, what a weekend.
> All I can say is, what a **trap** that was!
> Who knew a car ride could be like that?
> Even stopping for **gals** was a thing.

What I mean to say is that you're a true
fiend!

But what you meant to say was:

Hey,

I'm back home. Wow, what a weekend.
All I can say is, what a **trip** that was!
Who knew a car ride could be like that?
Even stopping for **gas** was a thing.

What I mean to say is that you're a true
friend!

Since all the misspelled words in the first email are actual words, spell check didn't flag them as wrong. So instead of thanking a friend for a cool time, you sent off an email saying the trip and your friend sucked. Oops.

So please, use spell check to catch *some* of your mistakes. But also take the time to look over your work. After all, you took the time to write it, so you may as well give it that little bit of extra love.

Words that are alike may be a pain, but don't let them rain on your writing

Ever feel as though certain words are just trying to confound you? The wily twerps are just similar enough to make it tough to choose between them.

Here are 15 of the most commonly confused words. I've included definitions and examples, along with tips on how to choose wisely between them.

affect vs. effect

Although both **affect** and **effect** can be used as nouns and verbs, people tend to confuse the verb **affect** when it means "to influence" with the noun **effect** when it means "result."

affect:

a) If you want to say "to influence" then use **affect.** In this case, **affect** is always a *verb.*

Wearing puce didn't seem to **affect** the bridesmaids' good cheer.

180

b) Although it's rare, you can also use **affect** as a noun, when it means "an aspect of an emotion." This is not the form of **affect** that generally causes confusion, but it's good to know your options.

> Some psychiatrists are doing research into the **affects** displayed by bridesmaids wearing hideous outfits.

effect:

a) If you want to say "a result" then use **effect.** In this case, **effect** is always a *noun.*

> You'd think wearing puce would have a big **effect** on the bridesmaids' good cheer.

b) It's much less common, but you can also use **effect** as a verb, meaning "bring about or cause." This isn't the form that gets confused with **affect,** but again, it's good to know your choices.

> Some psychiatrists have suggested medicating the brides when they pick the bridesmaids' gown to see if it would **effect** any change in their hideous choices.

Tip:

When trying to choose between the verb **affect** when it means "to influence" and the noun **effect** when it means "result," try this.

1. Isolate **effect-affect** from any adjectives or helping words.
2. Put the word **an** in front of **effect-affect.** If it makes sense, you need **effect,** the noun. If it doesn't, you need **affect,** the verb.

> Wearing puce didn't seem ~~to~~ **an affect** the bridesmaids' good cheer.

*(Using **an** doesn't make sense, so the verb **affect** is correct.)*

> You'd think wearing puce would have ~~a big~~ **an effect** on the bridesmaids' good cheer.

*(Using **an** makes sense, so the noun **effect** is correct.)*

among vs. between

among:

Use **among** when you're talking about *three or more things*.

The bride had a hard time choosing **among** *hats, parasols, and gloves* for the bridesmaids, so she chose them all.

between:
Use **between** when you're talking about *two things*.

The bride had a hard time choosing **between** *hats and parasols* for the bridesmaids, so she chose them both.

Tip:
On standardized tests, this is one of those nitpicky things they love to nail you with.

amount vs. number and fewer vs. less

number and **fewer:**
Use **number** and **fewer** to refer to *things that you can count.*

There are a **number** of *brides* who pick decent bridesmaids' dresses.

However, there are **fewer** *brides* with good taste than one would hope.
(You can count brides.)

amount and **less:**

Use **amount** and **less** to refer to *undefined things that you can't count.*

> What **amount** of *booze* do you think the bridesmaids drank to look happy in those dresses?

> Since they're still vertical, I'm guessing they drank **less** *booze* than we would have in their situation.

(You can't count booze.)

Still confused? Look at it this way:

> You have an **amount** of *hair,* but you have a **number** of *strands of hair.*

*(**Hair** is kind of undefined, but you can count individual **strands.**)*

> You throw an **amount** of *rice,* but you throw a **number** of *grains of rice.*

*(Again, **rice** is very nonspecific, whereas you can count individual **grains.**)*

bring vs. take

bring:

Use **bring** for things *coming toward*.

> Please remember to **bring** some pointy
> stakes with you for the vampire hunt.

take:

Use **take** for things *going away*.

> After the hunt, **take** the guts-encrusted
> stakes home with you for a good wash.

can vs. may

Teachers love to torment students with this one. Does this
sound familiar?

> **Student:** "Can I go to the bathroom?"
> **Teacher:** "I don't know. Can you?"

can:

Can means that you are *able* to do something.

> "Since the brains didn't come out of my
> jeans after that last battle, **can** I buy a
> new pair?" he asked.
> *(He is asking if he's able to buy a new pair, as*

though he doesn't know if he has the money or isn't sure he knows how to go about it.)

may:

May means that you want *permission* to do something.

> "Since the brains didn't come out of my jeans after that last battle, **may** I buy a new pair?" he asked.

(Now, he's asking for permission—he has the money and knows how to buy the jeans, but he doesn't know if he has permission to buy them.)

different from vs. different than

The majority of the time, use **different from,** not **different than.**

different from:

Use **different from** when you're contrasting things.

> He found it surprising that vampire guts were **different from** zombie guts.

different than:

Using **different than** is frowned upon by many grammar experts. If you do want to use it, then proceed with caution. The only time you may use **different than** is when it's followed by a clause.

> Due to putrefaction, zombie guts are **different than** they were when the zombies were still human.

*(Notice that **different than** is followed by the clause "they were when the zombies were still human.")*

Tip:

If you have any doubt about which one to use, stick with **different from.**

dragged vs. drug

As I mentioned in Thing 2, this mistake is just painful and should be avoided.

dragged:

Dragged is the past tense of the verb **to drag,** meaning "to haul" or "to move slowly."

> **Yes:** When we **dragged** the body to my trunk, my hair got totally messed up.

> **Yes:** I can't believe I got **dragged** into

helping out when I was having such a good hair day.

drug:

Drug is a noun meaning "a chemical substance" or a verb meaning "to give a chemical substance." It is *not* the past tense of the verb **to drag.**

> **No:** When we **drug** the body to my trunk, my hair got totally messed up.

> **Seriously, no:** I can't believe I got **drug** into helping out when I was having such a good hair day.

> **Yes:** I'm going to need a **drug** to get rid of the massive headache I've got from this mess.

Tip:

Unless you're writing dialogue where you want your character to sound a certain way, just say no to **drug** as the past tense of **dragged.**

e.g. vs. i.e.

e.g.:

Use **e.g.** when you want to say "for example."

A good hair day takes a lot of effort, **e.g.,** blow drying, curling, gelling, and hair spraying.

i.e.:

Use **i.e.** when you want to say "in other words."

Of course, his hair was immune to the weather, **i.e.,** it never even moved.

Tip:

In text, it's usually better to limit the use of abbreviations like e.g. and i.e. Try to save them for things like parenthetical remarks, but even then, use them sparingly.

farther vs. further

farther:

When you're talking about a *physical distance,* choose **farther.**

I think my hair frizzed because we walked much **farther** than I anticipated.

further:

Choose **further** when you want to say "more" or talk

about a nonphysical distance.

> He said there was no reason for **further** worry about my hair because I could fix it when we got back.

> It turned out that couldn't have been **further** from the truth, because he tried to shoot me after I helped him dispose of the evidence.

wary vs. weary

wary:

To be **wary** is to be cautious.

> I felt **wary** about the situation but I decided I was being silly to feel so nervous and went with him anyway.

weary:

To **be weary** is to be tired.

> However, walking that far made me really **weary** and I couldn't wait to get home and take a bath.

imply vs. infer

imply:

To **imply** is "to hint." Choose **imply** when you're talking about *giving out* information.

> He **implied** that there'd be a big reward if I'd go along with his nefarious plan.

infer:

To **infer** is "to pick up the hint." Choose **infer** when you're talking about *taking in* information and figuring it out.

> Silly me, I **inferred** from what he said that I'd be getting a monetary reward, not going to my just rewards.

irregardless vs. regardless

irregardless:

You should put this word in the same category as using "drug" as the past tense of "to drag." Don't do it. Irregardless is slang and you should not use it in your writing, unless you're writing dialogue.

regardless:

Stick with **regardless.** It means "heedless; in spite of."

> **No:** Irregardless of the situation, it's just rude to shoot someone when they're having a bad hair moment.

> **Yes:** Regardless of the situation, it's just rude to shoot someone when they're having a bad hair moment.

lay vs. lie

Telling **lay** and **lie** apart gets a bit confusing because the past tense of **lie** is also **lay.**

lay:

The verb **lay** means "to set, put, or place." You always need an object after this verb, telling you what was set, put, or placed.

Present	Past	**Past Participle** *(used with a helping verb)*
lay	laid	laid (has laid, had laid, etc.)

Present: I usually **lay** my purse on the ground before combat.

Past: I **laid** my purse on the ground and then I remembered the hairspray in it.

Past Participle: I **had laid** my purse on the ground before I remembered that there was a can of hairspray in it.

*(**My purse** is the object of **lay** because it tells you what is being put on the ground.)*

lie:

a) The verb **lie** means "to recline." You do not need an object after the verb **lie.**

Present	Past	Past Participle *(used with a helping verb)*
lie	lay	lain (had lain, had lain, etc.)

Present: He wanted me to **lie** on the ground while he decided what to do with me.

Past: When I **lay** down to sleep last night I had no idea that I'd be in this situation today.

Past Participle: I found myself wishing I **had lain** down and had a nap so that at least I wouldn't have such gnarly bags under my eyes in addition to my messed up hair.

People tend to confuse **lie** meaning "to recline" with **lay** meaning "to place." However, there's another verb form of **lie** that can add to the confusion.

b) The verb **lie** can also mean "not to tell the truth" or "say something untrue."

Present	Past	Past Participle *(used with a helping verb)*
lie	lied	lied (has lied, had lied, etc.)

Present: I can't **lie.** What I actually meant to do was to give my hair one last spritz, so that no matter what he decided, I wouldn't look totally horrendous.

Past: Of course, since he **lied** to me about his intentions, I don't feel bad that I accidentally sprayed him, too.

Past Participle: If he **hadn't lied** to me when he got me involved in his plans, I wouldn't have laughed so hard when he got a mouthful of hairspray.

tenant vs. tenet

Beware the Internet! People have been confusing these terms on the Internet a lot. I'm all for using a good vocabulary, but it's much more effective if you're using it correctly.

tenant:
A **tenant** is "an occupant."

Each **tenant** of the Superhero Suites is responsible for the upkeep of his own superhero costume.

tenet:
A **tenet** is "a principle or belief."

No: Neatness is a major **tenant** of her superhero philosophy.

Yes: Neatness is a major **tenet** of her superhero philosophy.

than vs. then

than:

Use **than** for comparisons.

> Do you think that Ironman is a better superhero **than** Batman?

then:

Use **then** when you want to show time.

> During a battle, if you notice that you've crimped your cape, it's suggested that you finish your fight, **then** smooth out the wrinkles.

Don't let confusing words get you down. I suggest figuring out which words tend to mess you up the most, and then keeping an eye out for them when you edit your writing.

‒ 36 ‒

Similar-sounding words are the sirens of sentences. They sound enticing, but will inevitably lead your sentence into the rocks

From the TV show *Castle:*

> **Detective Beckett** *(reading aloud a message scrawled on the face of a murder victim):* Psycho The Rapist Your Out of Time?
> **Medical Examiner:** Looks like a patient lost their patience.
> **Castle** *(a writer):* Also his command of grammar. "Your" should be "you" apostrophe "r-e" as in "you are." That's not even a tough one, not like when to use who or whom.

> > ~*Castle*, "The Double Down," season two, episode 2, written by David Grae

I'm with Castle. **Your** and **you're** are not really all that tough, but other homophones can be.

Homophones are words that sound alike, but they're spelled differently and have different meanings. Mixing them up is painfully common.

Even if you know the difference, it's easy to make a mistake with homophones when you're typing fast, like typing "its" instead of "it's." Spell check can't help you, either. It doesn't catch this kind of mistake because technically the word isn't misspelled. For that reason, I recommend making homophone patrol part of your editing process. Keeping an eye out for homophone mistakes when you look over your work can save you embarrassment.

How do you tell homophones apart? Here's a list of some of the most common offenders, along with definitions and examples.

assure vs. ensure vs. insure

assure:
> to tell with confidence; to promise; to convince

> We **assure** all cadets that we make visiting an alien planet as risk-free as possible.

ensure:

to make sure or certain; to guarantee

> However, it's impossible for us to
> **ensure** that everyone going to an alien
> planet will return alive, whole, and still
> human.

insure:

to issue an insurance policy

> As a result, we suggest that cadets fully
> **insure** themselves with life, property,
> and health policies, just in case.

capital vs. capitol

capital:

Capital has many definitions. Here are a few of the
most common ones. Most of the time you will need
to use **capital** not **capitol.** Think of it this way: If you
want to get an "a" go with capital.

1) the seat of government for a city, state, or nation
2) wealth; assets
3) a capital letter

1) Should you visit the **capital** of the planet, please wear your dress uniform.

2) When visiting alien cultures, we suggest that you refrain from investing any **capital** until you've cleared it with the Alien Assets Department.

3) In lieu of last year's unfortunate misunderstanding, please verify the meaning and use of all **capital** letters before committing anything to writing in an alien language.

capitol:

a government building

This word has very limited usage. Use **capitol** with an "o" only when you're referring to a government building, or a name that refers to government buildings, like Capitol Hill.

Please remember that spitting from the top of an alien **capitol** may be construed as a declaration of war.

cent vs. scent vs. sent

cent:

a penny

> Cadets are reminded that accepting any alien money, even a few **cents,** can have many unfortunate results.

scent:

odor; aroma; the way something smells

> No matter how enticing their **scent,** please don't sniff the aliens. It's considered rude.

sent:

transmitted; conveyed to a destination

> Space cadets breaking the rules will immediately be **sent** back to their home planets.

cereal vs. serial

cereal:

an edible grain; breakfast food

Many new space cadets prefer familiar foods for breakfast, like **cereal.**

serial:

a) something published in installments at regular intervals

However, cadets are encouraged to read the nutritional bulletin *Breakfast Bugs*, published as a **serial,** and incorporate its suggestions into their diet.

b) sequential; in a series; in installments or successive parts

After breakfast, cadets will report to their History of Technology class where they will study archaic technology, like **serial** ports.

cite vs. sight vs. site

cite:

to quote

On an alien mission, it is considered bad form to **cite** rules and regulations to your alien hosts.

sight:
vision; a view or glimpse

> On your mission, if the **sight** of the aliens startles you, please do not gasp and point.

site:
position or location

> A surprising number of planets exhibit nothing but rocks at the **site** where you beam down to the surface.

complement vs. compliment

complement:
a) something that completes

> The pirate bought the cutlass as a **complement** to his knife so that he could fight two-handed if need be.

b) to complete

With the big battle coming up, the pirate wanted to **complement** his existing fighting equipment.

compliment:
praise; admiration

From the **compliment** the captain gave him, the pirate knew the cutlass was a good choice.

desert vs. dessert

desert:
a) a dry area with little vegetation

After the unremitting moistness of the sea, the dry **desert** was a welcome respite to the pirates.

b) to leave or abandon

Debarking the ship was always dangerous because if the captain was in a bad mood, he might just set sail and **desert** them.

dessert:

a dish that's usually sweet, like cake, ice cream, or fruit, generally served at the end of a meal

But the juicy meats and sweet **desserts** awaiting them in the oasis lured them away from the ship.

discreet vs. discrete

discreet:

careful with conduct or speech; prudent; confidential

All the pirates knew that being **discreet** about the pirate treasure was the key to staying alive.

discrete:

separate; distinct

Spill the secret, and the captain would chop your body into **discrete** chunks and feed it to the sharks.

Tip:

The difference between *discrete* and *discreet* is another

one of those things you see on standardized tests a lot.

its vs. it's

This is the kind of little mistake that's bound to get you noticed for the wrong reason. People tend to look for this kind of error because it's so common. Unfortunately, they tend not to forgive it even though they see it so often—quite the opposite, in fact.

its:

Its is a possessive pronoun meaning "belonging to it." Remember that possessive pronouns do not need an apostrophe to show possession. *(For more on apostrophes, see Thing 22.)*

> Sometimes a pirate captain tries to hide the treasure from his crew, preferring to keep **its** location a secret.

it's:

It's is the contraction for "it is" or "it has." If you can swap "it is" or "it has" in place of the **its** in your sentence, then you should be using **it's,** so add that apostrophe!

> However, of all people, a pirate captain should know **it's** not a great idea to try to swindle pirates.

(it is not)

> **It's** been the cause of many a pirate captain's grisly death.

(it has been)

let's vs. lets

This is another one of those extremely common and, therefore, extremely irksome errors. Be careful not to let it sneak past you!

let's:
Let's is the contraction for "let us." If you can replace the **lets** in your sentence with "let us," then you should be using **let's.**

> **Let's** see how the wenches feel about pirates and treasure.

(let us)

lets:
   allows

>   That tavern **lets** pirates hang out with
>   the wenches.

loose vs. lose

loose:
   not tight; free from restraint

>   The **loose,** flowing pirate shirt has
>   caused more than one wench to swoon
>   with desire.

lose:
   a) to be defeated

>   Wenches have also been known to
>   swoon over the tall tales the pirates
>   tell, where they never **lose** a battle and
>   always get the gold.

   b) to mislay or misplace

>   It's amazing how many wenches
>   manage to **lose** their keys and require

a pirate's assistance in getting into their
rooms.

passed vs. past

Passed and **past** are confusing because the definitions
that have to do with traveling **past** something or going
beyond something are so similar to **passed** meaning "went
by." When choosing between **past** and **passed,** you'll have
to pay attention to both the definition and the part of speech.
The main thing to remember is that you can't use **past** as a
verb.

passed:
a) past tense of the verb **to pass** meaning "went by"

When the bank robbers **passed** us
riding the camel, we burst into laughter.

b) completed with a satisfactory grade

With their horses gone, the robbers'
choices were limited and the camel
must've been the only thing that
passed their inspection.

past:
  a) noun; time gone by

> In the **past,** the robbers might've been able to get away on foot, but they were clever enough to know that our current marshal has a good horse.

b) preposition; beyond in time
In this case, if you can substitute **after** for **past,** you're using the right word.

> The robbers were worried because it was already **past** two and they were running out of time.

c) preposition; beyond in space, position, or direction
In this case, try substituting **beyond** for **past.**

> When we looked **past** the bank, we could see that the robbers had already ridden **past** the general store and were heading toward us.

d) adverb; so as to pass by or beyond
In this case, use **past** to modify a verb. In the example

below, **past** modifies the verb **rode.**

The robbers rode **past.**

premier vs. premiere

premier:

a) a prime minister or chief officer

The bank robbers were smart to rob the bank when so many people were in town to celebrate the visit from the French **premier.**

b) first in importance; leading

As the **premier** bank robbers in the area, they had the experience to know that they needed to hit the bank while the marshal was distracted.

premiere:

the opening of a film, play, and so forth

The robbers waited to start the robbery until the marshal and all the visiting dignitaries were attending the **premiere** of the play at the town's new theater.

principal vs. principle

principal:
a) chief; head or chief of a school

> The high school **principal** was outside the theater smoking his pipe when he heard the commotion from the robbery.

b) of most importance

> He realized his **principal** duty was to notify the marshal without alerting the premier and the other officials.

principle:
belief; rule

> Since he made it a **principle** to remain calm and dignified at all times, he had no trouble keeping his composure as he approached the marshal.

Tip:

I used to confuse these two a lot until one of my acquaintances taught me this trick: The princi*pal* is my pal.

shear vs. sheer

shear:
to cut

> Meanwhile, the bank robbers were having a hard time riding the camel because someone had decided to **shear** its mane and they had nothing to hold on to.

sheer:
thin and see-through

> Further complicating the matter, the lead robber's bandana, though worn with age, wasn't threadbare enough to be **sheer,** so when it slipped over his eyes, he couldn't really see where they were going.

stationary vs. stationery

stationary:
not moving; standing still

> When the marshal caught up to the
> robbers, they were cursing and prodding
> the **stationary** camel, which stubbornly
> refused to budge as it nibbled on the
> hedge it had found.

stationery:
writing paper; writing materials

> With everyone eager to write their
> friends about the camel caper, the
> general store nearly ran out of
> **stationery.**

their vs. there vs. they're

their:
a possessive pronoun meaning "belonging to them"

> When the cashiers standing nearby
> saw that my Petunia wasn't going to let
> go of our clerk's pants, they left **their**

registers to come and help.

there:
a) a location or place

> Of course, it would've been better if
> they'd just stayed **there** and let me
> handle the situation.

b) for starting a sentence or clause

> **There** were so many people involved
> that the situation just got worse.

they're:
They're is the contraction for "they are." If you can
replace the **there** or **their** in your sentence with "they
are," then you should be using **they're.**

> I know that people think **they're**
> helping when they jump into a fray, but
> sometimes **they're** really not.

threw vs. through

threw:
past tense of the verb "to throw"; hurled; tossed

> One of the cashiers grabbed a doggie bone and **threw** it at Petunia, hoping to distract her.

through:

in one side and out the other

> As the doggie bone came winging **through** the air, I could see the cashier's aim was off.

to vs. too vs. two

to:

a) toward; in the direction of

> I wish the cashier had thrown the bone **to** me so that I could grab it, but instead it thwacked our clerk in the head.

b) with the infinitive form of verbs, like "to pry"

> While the clerk yelled at the cashier, I leaned over **to pry** Petunia from her posterior position.

too:
also

> I pulled Petunia away, but unfortunately, a chunk of the clerk's pants came away, too.

two:
one plus one, a set

> Of course, my sweet Petunia didn't bite the clerk's skin, but she did manage to rip **two** large holes in the patootie of his pants.

weather vs. whether

weather:
the state of the atmosphere

> When the balloons floated away with the cake table, the windy **weather** helped keep the table aloft.

whether:
if; either

> We couldn't decide **whether** we should try to shoot down the balloons or wait for the cake table to land on its own.

who's vs. whose

who's:

Who's is a contraction for "who is." If you can replace the **whose** in your sentence with "who is" then you should be using **who's**.

> But really, **who's** going to have good enough aim to hit a bunch of bobbing balloons without tipping the table and causing the cake to fall?

whose:

the possessive form of "who"

> Uncle Pete, **whose** job it was to follow the floating table, reported that somehow the table remained level and the cake was still intact.

yore vs. you're vs. your

yore:

olden days; time long past

> I found myself longing for the days of **yore** when they didn't have to worry about runaway balloon tables because they didn't have helium balloons.

you're:

You're is the contraction for "you are." If you can replace the **yore** or **your** in your sentence with "you are," then you should be using **you're.**

> You think **you're** totally prepared for the party, and then the balloons sneak off with the cake.

your:

possessive form of "you," meaning "belonging to you"

> How are you supposed to prepare for balloons stealing **your** cake?

From the same episode of *Castle* with which we began Thing 36:

> **Castle:** It's not like you're leaving yourself a note, you know, to buy bread on the way home. You're writing on a person you just murdered. You're trying to make a point. A point you care a great deal about, presumably, because you just killed someone to make it. So how do you not make sure that you're using the proper language to make that point?

I have to agree with Castle. If you're going to the trouble of writing something down (not on a corpse!), you should take the time to do it correctly. That means keeping an eye on those pesky homophones.

‒ 37 ‒

Is it one word or two? A space in the wrong place changes everything

Is the word you want supposed to be one word or two? Be careful, because the tiny space splitting your word also changes its meaning.

a lot vs. alot

a lot:
many; a great deal
This should *always be two words*. People often think **a lot** should be one word, but that isn't correct.

> The lead guitarist lost **a lot** of hair when they had to cut him free from his mic stand.

alot:
Don't use **alot**. It's not a real word.

all ready vs. already

all ready:

Use two words when you want to say "all are ready."

> The band's crew were **all ready** to leave the guitarist's hair an uneven mess because it made them giggle when they looked at him.

("All are ready to leave" makes sense.)

already:

early; before the expected time

Use one word when you want to talk about time.

> Much to the crew's dismay, the guitarist had **already** booked his hairdresser to meet him the next day.

all right vs. alright

all right and alright:

These words mean the same thing: "satisfactory."

The bottom line is that **all right** is preferable because most people won't accept the colloquial **alright.**

Always use **all right** for formal writing. You can get away with **alright** sometimes in informal writing.

> The guitarist decided that so long as he used even more hairspray, he looked **all right** with shorter hair.

all together vs. altogether

These poor guys get butchered a lot!

all together:
all at the same time; all at once
Use **all together** when you want to refer to a group doing something at the same time.

> The rest of the band decided to approach the guitarist **all together,** for a hairspray intervention.

altogether:
entirely; completely; wholly
Use **altogether** when you want an adverb to answer the question **how.**

> They told the guitarist that his hairspray

usage was **altogether** out of control,
forming a noxious cloud around him that
choked them onstage.

any more vs. anymore

any more:
something additional or extra

> Even the guitarist's hairstylist insisted
> his hair had so much cumulative buildup
> that he didn't need **any more** hairspray
> for at least a year.

anymore:
any longer; nowadays
If you can substitute "nowadays" for **any more,** or
the **any more** answers the question "when," then you
should be using **anymore** instead.

> The band members told the guitarist
> that the hairspray had become
> an addiction and he didn't need it
> **anymore.**

a part vs. apart

a part:

Use two words when you want to talk about a portion of something, or a role in a play, movie, and so on.

> The guitarist was happy being **a part** of the band. But he wasn't swayed until that night while he was playing **a part** of his guitar solo.

apart:

Use **apart** when you want to talk about being separate or detached.

> The band stood **apart,** safely out of range, and watched in amazement as the smoke started drifting from the guitarist's hair.

a while vs. awhile

a while:

Use **a while** when you want to say "for a time" but there's already a prepositional phrase that starts with "for."

> His bandmates stood there, mesmerized, for **a while** until finally a roadie came out and dumped a bucket of water on the guitarist's head.

awhile:

Awhile means "for a time." Do not use **awhile** after a prepositional phrase that starts with "for" because then what you're really saying is "for for a time." You can use **awhile** as one word when you can substitute the phrase "for a time" without winding up with "for" too many times.

> It may have taken him **awhile,** but after that last incident, the guitarist finally throttled back on his hairspray usage.

every day vs. everyday

every day:

Use **every day** when you can say "each day" instead.

> **Every day** since that truck with the crocodiles spilled on the freeway, we play "spot the crocodile" on our morning commute.

everyday:

usual; common; ordinary

Use **everyday** when you want to describe something as being common and ordinary.

> What should be a boring, **everyday** commute becomes downright creepy when you're crawling along, waiting for a crocodile to appear.

every one vs. everyone

every one:

Use **every one** when you can say "each one" instead.

> **Every one** of the passengers in the car gets really quiet when we creep along the area of the freeway now known as Crocodile Corridor.

everyone:

each and all

Use **everyone** when you can say "everybody" instead.

> That area of the freeway always slows down, and silly as it may be, **everyone** is nervous that somehow the crocodiles

will find a way to get into the car and attack.

may be vs. maybe

may be:

Use **may be** when you want to talk about a possible action.

> Getting out of the car to change a flat in Crocodile Corridor **may be** the stupidest thing we've ever done.

maybe:

perhaps

If you can substitute the word "perhaps" for the **may be** in your sentence, then you should be using **maybe** instead.

> **Maybe** it was dumb, but it gave us a great story to tell when we got to the office.

It's really easy to make this kind of mistake when you're in a hurry, and this is the kind of thing that spell check misses. Even when you're rushing, make a mental note to check for these errors so that you can be sure your writing says what you meant.

Check out these other books in the things *good* to know™ series:

41 Things To Know About Autism
(ISBN: 9781596525832, $9.99)

51 Things You Should Know Before Getting Engaged
(ISBN: 9781596525481, $9.99)

52 Things To Pick Up Your Poker Game
(ISBN: 9781596525917, $9.99)

99 Things to Save Money in Your Household Budget
(ISBN: 9781596525474, $9.99)

Contact Turner Publishing at (615) 255-2665
or visit turnerpublishing.com
to get your copies today!